Chefs' Special

Curries & Rice

Chefs' Special

Curries & Rice

Compiled by Master Chefs of India

Lustre Press
Roli Books

Gourmet Delight

In a land so rich in cultural heritage, it is but natural that the Indian cuisine is multifarious, offering a delight to both the eye and the palate. Its myriad flavours and cooking traditions find their roots in its historical influences. The Mughals revolutionised the art of Indian cooking with their delectable *biryanis* (an exquisite oven preparation with meat/vegetables, herbs and seasonings), *kormas* (a spicy meat or vegetarian preparation), *kebabs* and *tikkas* (meat and vegetables cooked in small pieces, usually on skewers) made in a *tandoor* (an oven made of mud and heated by a slow charcoal fire). The British Raj spawned an interesting Anglo-Indian gastronomic culture which is still eaten with relish. Different regions in India offer their own specialities with their very own taste, subtlety and aroma. The country's vast reservoir of spices made from its abundance of tropical herbs, serves as garnishing and contains medicinal and preservative properties. Indeed the range of the Indian cuisine can amaze even a connoisseur.

Curries & Rice brings you 32 curries—vegetarian and non-vegetarian—and 14 different ways to make *biryanis* and *pulaos* to tempt the palate. A few basic recipes of popular cooking ingredients, including *masalas*, Indian equivalents of foods given in each list of ingredients and a Glossary of Cooking Terms are valuable add-ons. A couple of *raitas*, a multi-purpose chutney and relishing *rotis* (pp. 102-107) serve as a complimentary fillip. And to provide a finishing touch, a sprinkling of 'handy hints' are added as sure-fire remedies to common culinary problems.

BASIC INDIAN RECIPES

Green Chilli Paste
Chop the required quantity of green chillies and process until pulped.

Garam Masala (for 450 gm)
Put 200 gm cumin, 35 gm peppercorns, 45 gm black cardamoms, 30 gm green cardamoms, 60 gm coriander seeds, 20 gm cloves, 20 gm cinnamon sticks, 15 gm bayleaves and 2 nutmegs in a processor and grind to a fine powder. Transfer to a bowl, add 20 gm mace powder and 30 gm ginger powder and mix well. Sieve and store in an airtight container.

Brown Onion Paste
Fry sliced onions over medium heat till brown. Drain excess oil and allow to cool. Process until pulped (using very little water, if required). Refrigerate in an airtight container.

Yoghurt
Boil milk and keep aside till lukewarm. Add 2 tsp yoghurt to the milk and mix well. Allow to ferment for 6-8 hours.

Red Chilli Paste
Chop red chillies and process until pulped.

Garam Masala

Yoghurt

Green Chilli Paste

Brown Onion Paste

Red Chilli Paste

Ginger/Garlic Paste
Soak ginger/garlic overnight. Peel, chop and process to pulp. Refrigerate in an airtight container.

Onion Paste
Peel and quarter onions and process until pulped. Refrigerate in an airtight container.

Tomato Purée
Peel, deseed and chop the tomatoes. Transfer to a pan, add 1 lt water, 8 cloves, 8 green cardamoms, 15 gm ginger, 10 gm garlic, 5 bayleaves and 5 peppercorns and cook on medium heat till the tomatoes are tender. Cool and process to a pulp.

Cottage Cheese (*Paneer*)
Heat 3 lt milk. Just before it boils, add 60 ml/4 tsp lemon juice or white vinegar. Strain the milk through a muslin cloth and hang for 2-3 hours to drain the whey and moisture.

Khoya
Boil milk in a wok (*kadhai*). Reduce heat and cook, stirring occasionally, till the quantity is reduced to half. Then stir constantly and scrape from all sides till a thick paste-like consistency is obtained. Allow to cool. *Khoya* is also called wholemilk fudge.

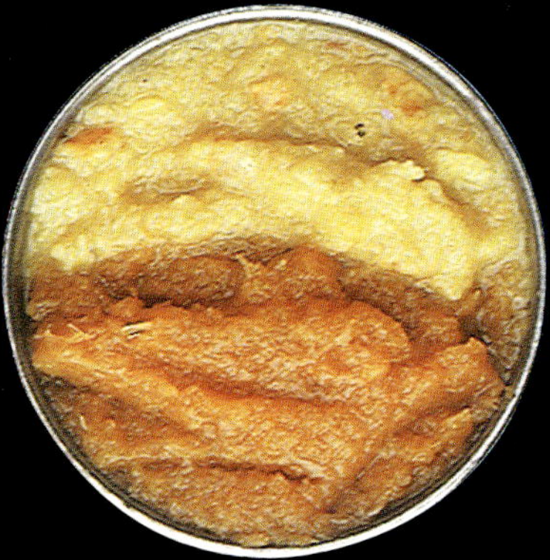

Ginger-Garlic Paste

Cottage Cheese

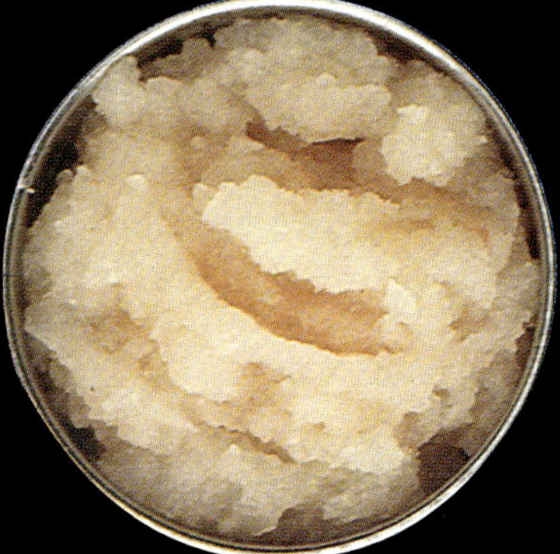

Onion Paste

Tomato Purée

Khoya

PULAO FLAVOURED WITH NUTS

Serves: 4   Preparation time: 40 minutes   Cooking time: 1 hour

Ingredients

Basmati rice *300 gm / 1 ½ cups*
Clarified butter (*ghee*) *200 gm / 1 cup*
Garam masala (p. 6) *10 gm / 2 tsp*
Water *450 ml / 2 ¼ cups*
Saffron (*kesar*) *3 gm / ½ tsp*
Warm milk *100 ml / ½ cup*
Cashewnuts *(kaju)*, broken, fried *60 gm / 4 tbsp*
Walnuts *(akhrot)*, fried *60 gm / 4 tbsp*
Almonds *(badam)*, fried *60 gm / 4 tbsp*
Peanuts *(moongphali)*, fried *60 gm / 4 tbsp*
Pistachios *(pista)*, fried *60 gm / 4 tbsp*
Raisins *(kishmish)*, fried *60 gm / 4 tbsp*
Rose water *(gulab jal) 15 ml / 1 tbsp*
Onions, fried *100 gm / ½ cup*

Method

1. Soak rice in sufficient water for 30 minutes. Drain and keep aside.

2. Heat clarified butter in a pan and add the garam masala. Sauté till it crackles.

3. Add the rice and fry till a pleasing aroma emanates. Add 450 ml water and boil till three-fourths cooked. Drain and keep aside. Soak saffron in warm milk.

4. In a pot (*handi*), sprinkle some saffron mixture. Spread a layer of rice and dry fruits, then add the remaining saffron mixture, rose water and fried onions. Seal the pot *(handi)* with aluminum foil.

5. Cook on very low heat (*dum*) for 30 minutes. Remove from heat and serve hot.

BROCCOLI AND CARROT PULAO

Serves: 4-5   Preparation time: 5 minutes   Cooking time: 30 minutes

Ingredients

Basmati rice *400 gm / 2 cups*
Broccoli florets *(hari phool gobi)*, small *150 gm / ¾ cup*
Carrots *(gajar)*, diced, parboiled *100 gm / ½ cup*
Oil *30 ml / 2 tbsp*
Cumin *(jeera)* seeds *8 gm / 1 ½ tsp*
Bayleaf *(tej patta) 1*
Cloves *(laung) 3*
Black pepper *(kali mirch) 5 gm / 1 tsp*
Salt to taste
Water *1 lt / 5 cups*

Method

1. Clean, wash and soak the rice in sufficient water for 10 minutes. Drain and keep aside.

2. Heat oil in a heavy-bottomed pan. Sauté the cumin seeds, bayleaf, cloves, and black pepper till they crackle. Add the carrots, broccoli and salt and stir-fry for 3-4 minutes.

3. Remove; discard the whole spices; keep the vegetables aside.

4. Boil 1 lt water in a separate pot; cook the rice until done and drain excess water.

5. Gently fold in the cooked vegetables into the rice and transfer to a serving platter. Serve hot.

LEMON RICE

Serves: 4   Preparation time: 5 minutes   Cooking time: 25-35 minutes

Ingredients

Basmati rice or any long-grain variety *100 gm / ½ cup*
Water *400-480 ml / 2-2 ⅔ cups*
Salt *5 gm / 1 tsp*
Oil / clarified butter *(ghee)* *45 ml / 3 tbsp*
Cashewnuts *(kaju)*, chopped *75 gm / ½ cup*
Black gram, split *(dhuli urad dal)*, *7 gm / ½ tbsp*
Mustard *(rai)* seeds *5 gm / 1 tsp*
Red chillies, whole *2-3*
Turmeric *(haldi)* powder *3 gm / ½ tsp*
Lemon juice *80 ml / ⅓ cup*
Green coriander *(hara dhaniya)*, coarsely chopped *45 gm / 3 tbsp*
Coconut *(nariyal)*, fresh, shredded *25 gm / 5 tsp*

Method

1. Wash and soak the rice in water for 10 minutes. Drain and keep aside.
2. Boil water in a heavy-bottomed pan. Stir in rice, salt and 7 ml / ½ tbsp oil. Cover tightly, reduce heat and simmer without stirring until the rice is fluffy and tender and the water is fully absorbed. Keep aside.
3. Heat remaining oil in a small pan. Stir-fry the cashewnuts until golden brown. Spoon cashewnuts over the cooked rice and replace cover.
4. Raise the heat slightly. Sauté the split black gram and mustard seeds. Add the red chillies and remove from heat.
5. Gently fold in the sautéed mixture along with turmeric powder, lemon juice, coriander and coconut into the cooked rice until well mixed.
6. Serve hot, with plain yoghurt *(dahi)* (p. 6).

MUSHROOM PULAO

Serves: 2   Preparation time: 1 hour   Cooking time: 30-40 minutes

Ingredients

Black mushrooms *(guchi)* *30 gm / 2 tbsp*
Basmati rice *350 gm / 1 3/4 cups*
Oil *15 ml /1 tbsp*
Cinnamon *(dalchini)* stick *1*
Green cardamoms *(choti elaichi) 4*
Black cardamoms *(bari elaichi) 2*
Cloves *(laung) 4*
Bayleaves *(tej patta) 4*
Onion, sliced *45 gm / 3 tbsp*
Ginger-garlic *(adrak-lasan)* paste (p. 8) *10 gm / 2 tsp*
Vegetable stock *750 ml / 3 3/4 cups*
Salt to taste
Butter *100 gm / 1/2 cup*
Lemon *1/2*
Milk *60 ml / 4 tbsp*

Method

1. Soak the black mushrooms and Basmati rice in separate pans for 30 minutes. Drain and keep aside.
2. Cut the black mushrooms into small pieces.
3. Heat oil in a pot *(handi)*. Add the whole spices and sauté till they crackle. Add the onion and stir-fry till golden brown in colour.
4. Add the ginger-garlic paste dissolved in a little water and sauté further.
5. Stir in the vegetable stock and bring to a boil. Add salt, 90 gm butter and juice of half a lemon.
6. Add the rice and cook on medium heat, stirring occasionally. When the water is reduced to the level of the rice, sprinkle milk on top and cover with a wet cloth. Cook on very low heat for 15 minutes or until the rice is cooked.

7. Heat the remaining butter in a pan and sauté the black mushrooms for a few minutes. Remove and keep aside.

8. Remove the prepared rice to a serving dish and serve hot, garnished with fried mushrooms.

Milky Matter

If milk has got burnt slightly due to carelessness, a pinch of salt will take away the burnt smell.

JACKFRUIT PULAO

Serves: 4-5   Preparation time: 45 minutes   Cooking time: 30 minutes

Ingredients

Basmati rice *200 gm / 1 cup*
Jackfruit *(kathal)*, cleaned, cubed *250 gm / 1 ¼ cups*
Oil *200 ml / 1 cup*
Cloves *(laung) 4*
Cinnamon *(dalchini)* stick *1*
Bayleaf *(tej patta) 1*
Black cardamoms *(bari elaichi) 2*
Caraway seeds *(shahi jeera) 5 gm / 1 tsp*
Onions, chopped *50 gm / ¼ cup*
Ginger *(adrak)* paste (p. 8) *10 gm / 2 tsp*
Red chilli powder *3 gm / ½ tsp*
White pepper *(safed mirch)* powder *3 gm / ½ tsp*
Salt to taste
Water *500 ml / 2 ½ cups*

For the garnishing:

Cashewnuts *(kaju)*, chopped, fried *5 gm / 1 tsp*
Green coriander *(hara dhaniya)*, chopped *3 gm / ½ tsp*
Cream *30 gm / 2 tbsp*
Ginger *(adrak)*, julienned (long, thin strips) *3 gm / ½ tsp*
Green chillies, sliced, deseeded *5 gm / 1 tsp*
Lemon juice *15 ml / 1 tbsp*
Mace powder *(javitri) 3 gm / ½ tsp*
Onion, sliced, fried *1*

Method

1. Clean, wash and soak the rice for 30 minutes.
2. Heat oil in a wok *(kadhai)* till it starts smoking. Fry jackfruit cubes till light brown in colour. Drain oil and keep aside.
3. Reheat the same oil in a heavy pan. Add the cloves,

cinnamon stick, bayleaf, cardamoms and caraway seeds and sauté over medium heat until they begin to crackle.

4. Add chopped onions and sauté. Stir in the ginger paste and red chilli powder. Add the fried jackfruit, white pepper powder and salt. Cook for 3-4 minutes.

5. Stir in water along with drained rice. Bring to a boil, reduce heat and cook till rice is done.

6. Remove the lid and sprinkle cashewnuts, green coriander, cream, ginger, green chillies, lemon juice, mace powder and onion.

7. Seal the lid with dough, cook on very low heat *(dum)* for 10-15 minutes. Serve hot.

Keep the Rice Pearly White

While cooking pulao, add a few drops of lemon juice; the grains will remain separate and white.

VEGETABLE BIRYANI

(Highly seasoned vegetable rice)

Serves: 4-5   Preparation time: 45 minutes   Cooking time: 30 minutes

Ingredients

Basmati rice or any long-grain variety *200 gm / 1 cup*
Carrot *(gajar)*, diced, parboiled *20 gm / 4 tsp*
Cauliflower *(phool gobi)*, small pieces *20 gm / 4 tsp*
Green peas *(mattar)*, parboiled *20 gm / 4 tsp*
Mushrooms *(guchi)*, quartered *20 gm / 4 tsp*
Oil *60 ml / 4 tbsp*
Cloves (*laung*) *4*
Cinnamon (*dalchini*) stick, medium *1*
Bayleaf (*tej patta*) *1*
Green cardamoms (*choti elaichi*) *3*
Caraway seeds (*shahi jeera*) *5 gm / 1 tsp*
Onions, chopped *50 gm / ¼ cup*
Ginger *(adrak)* paste (p. 8) *10 gm / 2 tsp*
Red chilli powder *3 gm / ⅔ tsp*
White pepper *(safed mirch)* powder *2 gm / ½ tsp*
Salt to taste
Water *500 ml / 2 ½ cups*

For garnishing:

Green chillies, slit *5 gm / 1 tsp*
Onion, sliced, fried *10 gm / 2 tsp*
Mace (*javitri*) powder *2 gm / ½ tsp*
Lemon juice *15 ml / 1 tbsp*
Ginger *(adrak)*, julienned (long, thin strips) *3 gm / ⅔ tsp*
Cashewnuts *(kaju)*, fried golden *10*
Coriander *(hara dhaniya)*, chopped *5 gm / 1 tsp*
Cream *30 gm / 2 tbsp*

Method

1. Wash and soak the rice for 30 minutes.
2. Heat oil in a heavy-bottomed pan. Sauté the cloves, cinnamon stick, bayleaf, cardamoms and caraway seeds until they begin to crackle.
3. Add onions and stir-fry till transparent. Stir in the ginger paste, red chilli powder, all the vegetables along with white pepper and salt. Cook for 3-4 minutes.
4. Stir in the drained rice and water. Bring to a boil, lower heat, cover and cook till the rice is almost done.
5. Remove the lid, sprinkle slit green chillies, fried onions, mace powder, lemon juice, julienned ginger, cashewnuts, green coriander and cream.
6. Seal lid with dough and cook on very low heat for 10-15 minutes.
7. Serve hot, accompanied by yoghurt *(dahi)* (p. 6).

Insect-Free Rice

To avoid insects and worms in stored rice, add neem leaves, boric powder or camphor.

COTTAGE CHEESE PULAO

Serves: 4   Preparation time: 1 hour   Cooking time: 25 minutes

Ingredients

Basmati rice *350 gm / 1 ¾ cups*
Cottage cheese *(paneer)* (p. 8) *80 gm*
Salt to taste
Red chilli powder *3 gm / ½ tsp*
Cornflour *(makkai ka atta)* *10 gm / 2 tsp*
Oil *15 ml / 1 tbsp* + for frying
Cinnamon *(dalchini)* powder *10 gm / 2 tsp*
Green cardamoms *(choti elaichi) 4*
Black cardamoms *(bari elaichi) 2*
Cloves *(laung) 4*
Bayleaves *(tej patta) 4*
Onions, sliced *45 gm / 3 tbsp*
Ginger-garlic *(adrak-lasan)* paste (p. 8) *45 gm / 3 tbsp*
Vegetable stock *750 ml / 3 ¾ cups*
Salt *8 gm / 1 ½ tsp*
Butter *100 gm / ½ cup*
Lemon *½*
Milk *60 ml / 4 tbsp*

Method

1. Soak rice in sufficient water for 30 minutes; drain and keep aside.

2. Mash the cottage cheese. Add salt, red chilli powder and cornflour. Mix well and make small balls of the mixture. Heat oil in a pan and deep fry the cottage cheese balls to a light golden brown colour. Remove and keep aside.

3. Heat oil in a pot *(handi)*. Add the whole spices and sauté till they crackle. Add sliced onions and stir-fry

to a golden brown colour. Add ginger-garlic paste dissolved in water.

4. Stir vegetable stock and bring to a boil. Add salt, butter and juice of half a lemon. Add the rice and cook on medium heat, stirring occasionally.

5. When the water is reduced to the level of the rice, sprinkle milk on top. Cover with a wet cloth and cook on low heat *(dum)* for 15 minutes or until the rice is cooked.

6. Remove from heat and serve hot, garnished with fried cottage cheese balls.

Garnishing Tricks

For garnishing pulao, fry onions with a pinch of sugar. They will turn brown faster.

GUCHI BIRYANI

(Highly seasoned rice with mushrooms)

Serves: 4   Preparation time: 1 hour   Cooking time: 30 minutes

Ingredients

Rice *1 kg / 5 cups*
Mushrooms *(guchi)*, large *100 gm / ½ cup*

For the filling:

Cottage cheese (*paneer*) (p. 8), mashed *30 gm / 2 tbsp*
Cashewnuts *(kaju)*, chopped *10 gm / 2 tsp*
Raisins *(kishmish)*, chopped *10 gm / 2 tsp*
Ginger *(adrak)*, chopped *5 gm / 1 tsp*
Cumin (*jeera*) seeds *3 gm / ½ tsp*

For the curry:

Oil *100 ml / ½ cup*
Garam masala (p. 6), whole *10 gm / 2 tsp*
Onion paste (p. 8) *200 gm / 1 cup*
Yoghurt *(dahi)* (p. 6), hung *150 gm / ¾ cup*
Cashewnut *(kaju)* paste *30 gm / 2 tbsp*
Ginger-garlic *(adrak-lasan)* paste (p. 6) *30 gm / 2 tbsp*
Turmeric (*haldi*) powder *3 gm / ½ tsp*
Yellow chilli powder *5 gm / 1 tsp*
Salt to taste

Method

1. Clean the mushrooms and keep aside.
2. For the filling, mix together all the ingredients and fill the mushrooms with the prepared filling.
3. For the curry, heat oil in a pan. Add the garam masala and sauté till it crackles.
4. Add onion paste and cook till it leaves water. Stir

in all the other ingredients and cook for a few minutes. Remove and keep aside.

5. Boil rice in sufficient water till three-quarters done. Drain and keep aside.

6. In a pot (*handi*), spread alternate layers of rice, mushrooms and the prepared curry. Cover and cook on very low heat (*dum*) till the rice is done and the mushrooms are tender.

7. Remove from heat and serve hot.

Get the Best from Yoghurt

To set delicious and creamy yoghurt, use earthenware for best results.

PEA PULAO

Serves: 4-5 Preparation time: 5 minutes Cooking time: 30 minutes

Ingredients

Basmati rice *400 gm / 2 cups*
Fresh peas *(mattar)*, boiled *200 gm / 1 cup*
Oil *10 ml / 2 tsp*
Cumin (*jeera*) seeds *10 gm / 2 tsp*
Salt to taste
Water

Method

1. Clean, wash and soak the rice for 10 minutes.
2. Heat oil in a heavy-bottomed pan and sauté the cumin seeds till they crackle.
3. Add the boiled peas and salt. Stir-fry for a few minutes and set aside.
4. Put water to boil in a big pot and cook the rice. Drain excess water.
5. Gently fold the peas into the rice and serve hot, accompanied by any curry dish.

CHICKEN BIRYANI

(Highly seasoned rice with chicken)

Serves: 4   Preparation time: 1 hour 30 minutes   Cooking time: 30 minutes

Ingredients

Chicken, cut into pieces *1 kg*
Basmati rice *1 kg*
Yoghurt *(dahi)* (p. 6) *300 gm / 1 ½ cups*
Ginger-garlic *(adrak-lasan)* paste (p. 8) *45 gm / 3 tbsp*
Salt to taste
Yellow chilli powder *15 gm / 1 tbsp*
Garam masala (p. 6) *5 gm / 1 tsp*
Clarified butter (*ghee*) *250 gm / 1 ¼ cups*
Garam masala (p. 6), whole *20 gm / 4 tsp*
Onions, sliced *250 gm / 1 ¼ cups + 200 gm / 1 cup*
Mint *(pudina)*, chopped *20 gm / 4 tsp*
Green coriander *(hara dhaniya)*, chopped *30 gm / 2 tbsp*
Saffron (*kesar*) *2-3 gm / ½ tsp*
Milk *100 ml / ½ cup*
Chicken stock *4 lt / 20 cups*

Method

1. Marinate the chicken pieces with yoghurt, ginger-garlic paste, salt to taste, yellow chilli powder and garam masala.
2. Heat 150 gm clarified butter in a pot (*handi*). Add garam masala and onions. Sauté till golden brown. Pick out and add the chicken pieces and stir-fry till the water evaporates.
3. Stir in the rest of the marinade, mint and green

coriander. Cook on low heat till the chicken pieces are tender.

4. Make a mixture of saffron, 100 gm clarified butter and ½ cup of milk and keep warm.

5. Boil rice in chicken stock. Fry 200 gm onions in oil and keep aside.

6. In a pot (*handi*), arrange alternate layers of rice, chicken pieces, saffron mixture and fried onions.

7. Cover the pot with a wet cloth. Seal with lid and dough. Bake in a moderately hot oven for 15 minutes. Remove and serve hot.

Chatpatta Chutney

For a tasty chutney, grind 2 cucumbers, 1 tomato, a few cumin seeds, ginger and green chillies. Add salt and lime juice to taste.

Chicken Biryani ▶

ZAFRANI BIRYANI

(Chicken biryani seasoned with saffron)

Serves: 4-5   Preparation time: 50 minutes   Cooking time: 1 hour

Ingredients

Basmati rice or any long-grain variety *500 gm / 2 ½ cups*
Chicken *1 kg*
Yoghurt (*dahi*) (p. 6) *600 gm / 3 cups*
Saffron (*kesar*) *½ gm / a pinch*
Milk *100 ml / ½ cup*
Cream *50 gm / ¼ cup*
Mint (*pudina*) leaves *10 gm / 2 tsp*
Green coriander (*hara dhaniya*) *10 gm / 2 tsp*
Water *4 lt / 20 cups*
Bayleaves (*tej patta*) *2*
Green cardamoms (*choti elaichi*) *10*
Cloves (*laung*) *10*
Salt to taste
Butter (*makhan*), unsalted *150 gm / ¾ cup*
Black cardamoms (*bari elaichi*) *2*
Cinnamon (*dalchini*) sticks *4*
Mace (*javitri*) *5 gm / 1 tsp*
Caraway seeds (*shahi jeera*) *6 gm / 1 ⅓ tsp*
Onions, sliced *100 gm / ½ cup*
Ginger (*adrak*) paste (p. 8) *40 gm / 2 ⅔ tbsp*
Garlic (*lasan*) paste (p. 8) *40 gm / 2 ⅔ tbsp*
Red chilli powder *10 gm / 2 tsp*
Lemon juice *10 ml / 2 tsp*

Method

1. Clean, skin and cut the chicken into 8 pieces.
2. Wash the rice and soak for at least half an hour.
3. Whisk the yoghurt in a bowl and divide into two equal portions. Dissolve the saffron in warm milk and

cream. Add one portion of the yoghurt to it. Add the mint and green coriander to this.

4. Preheat oven to 150 °C / 300 °F.

5. In a saucepan, boil 4 lt water and add a bayleaf, 2 green cardamoms and 2 cloves. Add the washed rice and salt to taste. Boil for a few minutes until the rice is half cooked. Drain the rice with the whole spices and keep hot.

6. Heat butter in a pan, add the remaining whole spices and caraway seeds and sauté over medium heat. Add the onions and sauté until golden brown. Add the ginger and garlic pastes and red chilli powder and stir for 15 seconds.

7. Add the chicken and salt to taste and cook for a further 3-4 minutes.

8. Add the second portion of plain yoghurt along with approximately 200 ml water; stir and bring to a boil. Lower the heat and simmer until the chicken is almost done. Stir in lemon juice and check the seasoning.

9. Grease a large baking dish. Spread half the chicken mixture, sprinkle half the saffron/yoghurt/mint/coriander mixture over this. Now spread half the parboiled rice. Repeat the same process for the remaining half. Cover with a moist cloth and seal the dish with dough.

10. Slow-bake in the oven *(dum)* for 10-15 minutes.

11. Remove and serve hot, garnished with fried almonds.

MUTTON BIRYANI

(Highly seasoned mutton rice)

Serves: 4   Preparation time: 30 minutes   Cooking time: 1 hour

Ingredients

Mutton, cut into pieces *600 gm*
Rice *300 gm / 1 ½ cups*
Clarified butter (*ghee*) *150 gm / ¾ cup*
Yoghurt *(dahi)* (p. 6) *200 gm / 1 cup*
Red chilli powder *15 gm / 1 tbsp*
Ginger *(adrak)* paste (p. 8) *15 gm / 1 tbsp*
Asafoetida (*hing*) powder *5 gm / 1 tsp*
Cumin (*jeera*) powder *3 gm / ½ tsp*
Clove (*laung*) powder *3 gm / ½ tsp*
Black cardamom (*bari elaichi*) powder *3 gm / ½ tsp*
Vetivier (*kewda*) water *20 ml / 4 tsp*
Saffron (*kesar*) *3 gm / ½ tsp*
Milk *200 ml / 1 cup*

Method

1. Heat clarified butter in a pan. Add the mutton pieces and sauté till light brown. Add yoghurt, red chilli powder, ginger paste and asafoetida powder. Cook on low heat till the meat pieces are tender.

2. Stir in the cumin, clove and black cardamom powders.

3. Boil rice in sufficient water. Drain excess water and keep aside. Soak saffron in 200 ml milk.

4. In a greased, heavy-bottomed pan, spread a layer of half the rice, vetivier water, saffron milk and mutton pieces. Repeat the same process for the remaining half.

5. Cover and seal the pan; cook on very low heat *(dum)* for 30 minutes. Remove and serve hot.

LAMB BIRYANI

Serves: 4   Preparation time: 30 minutes   Cooking time: 1 hour 30 minutes

Ingredients

Lamb (cut into 1" cubes) *1 kg*
Basmati rice *400 gm / 2 cups*
Oil *100 ml / ½ cup*
Onions, chopped *120 gm / ½ cup*
Green cardamoms *(choti elaichi) 5*
Cloves *(laung) 2*
Cinnamon *(dalchini)* (1" stick) *1*
Yoghurt (*dahi*) (p. 6), whisked *120 gm / ½ cup*
Yellow chilli powder *5 gm / 1 tsp*
Salt to taste
Lamb stock *400 ml / 2 cups*
Mace *(javitri)* powder *a pinch*
Mint (*pudina*) leaves, chopped *5 gm / 1 tsp*
Ginger (*adrak*), chopped *30 gm / 2 tbsp*
Vetivier *(kewda)* a few drops
Cream *120 gm / ½ cup*
Butter, melted *45 gm / 3 tbsp*
Saffron *(kesar) a pinch*
Dough to seal dish
Ginger, julienned (long, thin strips) *5 gm / 1 tsp*

Method

1. Heat oil in a pan and sauté chopped onions. Add cardamoms, cloves and cinnamon in the oil till they crackle, then add lamb pieces and sauté.
2. Add yoghurt, yellow chilli powder and salt. Stir till dry. Add stock and cook till the meat is almost done.
3. In a separate pan, boil rice in plenty of water till the grains lengthen but are not fully cooked. Drain the water.
4. Remove the meat pieces from the curry and spread in a heat-proof casserole. Strain the curry. Reserve half the curry and pour the remaining over the meat.

Sprinkle mace, mint, chopped ginger, vetivier and half the cream over the meat.

5. Place half the rice on the meat pieces. Sprinkle the reserved cream, the reserved curry, the melted butter and saffron—crushed in a spoonful of water, over it.

6. Place the rest of the rice on top. Cover and seal lid with dough. Cook over very gentle heat for about 10-15 minutes. Remove from heat, garnish with julienned ginger.

7. Serve hot.

Soften with Beer

To tenderise meat and add flavour to it, marinate it for an hour in beer.

STIR-FRIED SPINACH WITH COTTAGE CHEESE

Serves: 4   Preparation time: 10-15 minutes   Cooking time: 25-30 minutes

Ingredients

Spinach (*palak*) *1 kg*
Cottage cheese (*paneer*) (p. 8), cubed *400 gm / 2 cups*
Oil *60 ml / 4 tbsp*
Cumin (*jeera*) seeds *5 gm / 1 tsp*
Garlic *(lasan)* cloves *10 gm / 2 tsp*
Whole red chillies *2*
Coriander *(dhaniya)* powder *3 gm / ½ tsp*
Cumin (*jeera*) powder *2 gm / ½ tsp*
Red chilli powder *3 gm / ½ tsp*
Salt to taste

Method

1. Blanch spinach, drain and chop coarsely.
2. Heat oil in a wok *(kadhai)*. Add cumin and garlic and sauté until the garlic changes colour. Add whole red chillies; stir for half a minute. Add spinach; stir-fry adding coriander powder, cumin powder and red chilli powder.
3. Add cottage cheese and stir-fry for 5 minutes. Season with salt.
4. Serve hot.

PALAK KOFTAS

(Curried spinach balls)

Serves: 4   Preparation time: 15 minutes   Cooking time: 20 minutes

Ingredients

For the gravy:

Oil *30 ml / 2 tbsp*
Cumin *(jeera)* seeds *2 ½ gm / ½ tsp*
Onion, chopped *1*
Ginger *(adrak)* paste (p. 8) *5 gm / 1 tsp*
Garlic *(lasan)* paste (p.8) *5 gm / 1 tsp*
Cashewnut *(kaju)* paste *30 gm / 2 tbsp*
Turmeric *(haldi)* powder *2 ½ gm / ½ tsp*
Red chilli powder *5 gm / 1 tsp*
Salt to taste
Tomatoes, chopped *240 gm / 1 ¼ cups*
Coriander leaves *(hara dhaniya)*, chopped *5 gm / 1 tsp*
Cream *15 gm / 1 tbsp*

For the *koftas*

Spinach *(palak) 175 gm*
Poppy seeds *(khus khus) 15 gm / 1 tbsp*
Cashewnuts *(kaju)*, broken *30 gm / 2 tbsp*
Coriander *(dhaniya)* powder *2 ½ gm / ½ tsp*
Cumin *(jeera)* powder *2 ½ gm / ½ tsp*
Red chilli powder *2 ½ gm / ½ tsp*
Salt to taste
Gram flour *(besan) 240 gm / 1 ¼ cups*
Oil for frying

Method

1. For the *koftas*, clean, wash and parboil spinach leaves. Cool, squeeze out water and mash the leaves.
2. Grind poppy seeds and cashewnuts to a paste.
3. Mix all remaining ingredients for the koftas, except

oil, with the cashewnut-poppy seed paste and spinach.

4. Divide the mixture into 8 portions and roll into round balls. Heat oil in a wok (*kadhai*) and deep fry the balls. Keep aside.

5. For the gravy, heat 2 tbsp oil in a wok (*kadhai*). Sauté cumin seeds. Add chopped onions and sauté till brown.

6. Add ginger and garlic pastes, cashewnut paste, turmeric, red chilli powder and salt. Fry for 2-3 minutes.

7. Add chopped tomatoes and fry for another 8-10 minutes. Add 120 ml / ½ cup water and simmer.

8. Before serving, add the *koftas* to the gravy and simmer for a few minutes. Transfer to a serving bowl and garnish with coriander leaves and cream.

No Go Without Tomatoes

Store tomatoes in the deep freezer
to keep them fresh for months.

SPICY BENGAL GRAM

Serves: 4-5   Preparation time: 45 minutes   Cooking time: 1 hour

Ingredients

Bengal gram, split (*chana dal*) *250 gm / 1 ¼ cups*
Water *1 ½ lt / 7 ½ cups*
Bayleaf (*tej patta*) *1*
Cinnamon (*dalchini*) stick *1*
Butter *40 gm / 2 ⅔ tbsp*
Onions, chopped *100 gm / ½ cup*
Garam masala (p. 6) *6 gm / 1 ⅓ tsp*
Ginger *(adrak)* paste (p. 8) *10 gm / 2 tsp*
Garlic *(lasan)* paste (p. 8) *10 gm / 2 tsp*
Tomatoes, skinned, chopped *60 gm / 4 tbsp*
Salt to taste
Green coriander *(hara dhaniya)*, chopped *5 gm / 1 tsp*

Method

1. Clean the gram, wash in water 3 or 4 times and soak for 30 minutes.
2. Boil water in a saucepan. Add the bayleaf, cinnamon stick and the drained gram; bring to a slow boil. Remove the scum from the top of the pan and simmer until the gram is completely cooked. Discard the bayleaf and cinnamon stick.
3. Heat butter in a pan and sauté the onions till they are soft and golden. Add the garam masala, ginger-garlic pastes and sauté over medium heat for 2-3 minutes.
4. Add the tomatoes, cooked gram and salt. Cover and cook for 2-3 minutes.
5. Serve hot, garnished with green coriander.

DUM ALOO BHOJPURI

(Slow-cooked potatoes, Bhojpuri style)

Serves: 4-5 Preparation time: 20 minutes Cooking time: 20 minutes

Ingredients

Potatoes, small, round *600 gm*
Clarified butter (*ghee*) *15 gm / 1 tbsp*
Onions, grated *80 gm / 5 $^1/_3$ tbsp*
Ginger *(adrak)* paste (p. 8)
30 gm / 2 tbsp
Garlic *(lasan)* paste (p. 8)
30 gm / 2 tbsp

For the filling:

Potatoes, boiled, grated
200 gm / 1 cup
Red chilli powder *10 gm / 2 tsp*
Turmeric(*haldi*) powder *5 gm / 1 tsp*
Garam masala (p. 6) *10 gm / 2 tsp*
Lemon juice *15 ml / 1 tbsp*
Salt to taste

For the curry:

Oil *50 ml / 3 $^1/_3$ tbsp*
Bayleaf (*tej patta*) *1*
Cinnamon (*dalchini*) sticks *2*
Cloves (*laung*) *6*
Green cardamoms (*choti elaichi*) *6*
Caraway seeds (*shahi jeera*) *3 gm / $^2/_3$ tsp*
Yoghurt *(dahi)* (p. 6), whisked *150 gm / ¾ cup*

Method

1. Heat the clarified butter in a pan. Add half the grated onions, ginger and garlic pastes and fry for 4-5 minutes. Add grated potatoes, and half the red chilli powder, turmeric powder and garam masala. Season with half the lemon juice and salt. Keep aside.

2. Boil and peel the small potatoes. Scoop out centres and deep fry the shells till they are slightly crisp.

3. Fill each potato shell with the prepared potato mixture. Cover and keep aside.
4. Heat oil in a pan. Add bayleaf, cinnamon, cloves, green cardamoms, caraway seeds and fry until they begin to crackle.
5. Mix in the remaining onions, ginger and garlic pastes and stir-fry for 2-3 minutes.
6. Add turmeric powder and red chilli powder. Stir-fry over medium heat for 5-6 minutes. Stir in yoghurt. Cook till the liquids evaporate, stirring regularly. Season with the remaining garam masala and salt.
7. Arrange the stuffed potatoes in the pan. Sprinkle lemon juice, cover and cook for 3-4 minutes on very low heat.
8. Serve hot, garnished with julienned ginger, as an accompaniment to any Indian bread of choice (pp. 104-107).

Pushy Potatoes

To boil potatoes faster, add a little turmeric powder and oil to the water.

PANEER-DO-PIAZA

(Cottage cheese with onions)

Serves: 4-5   Preparation time: 10 minutes   Cooking time: 10 minutes

Ingredients

Cottage cheese *(paneer)*, cut into cubes *900 gm / 4 ½ cups*
Oil *60 ml / 4 tbsp*
Green cardamoms *(choti elaichi) 3*
Cumin *(jeera)* seeds *3 gm / ⅔ tsp*
Turmeric *(haldi)* powder *8 gm / 1 ⅔ tsp*
Red chilli powder *5 gm / 1 tsp*
Capsicums (Shimla *mirch*), cut into squares *150 gm / ¾ cup*
Button onions *300 gm / 1 ½ cups*
Tomatoes, cut into cubes *150 gm / ¾ cup*
Garam masala (p. 6) *15 gm / 3 tsp*
Salt to taste
Green coriander (*hara dhaniya*), chopped *15 gm / 3 tsp*
Lemon juice *10 ml / 2 tsp*

Method

1. Heat the oil in a pan. Add cardamoms and cumin seeds and sauté over medium heat until they begin to crackle. Add the turmeric and red chilli powder and sauté for 30 seconds.

2. Add the capsicums, button onions and tomatoes and sauté for another 30 seconds over high heat.

3. Add the cottage cheese cubes, garam masala and salt. Cook for 6 minutes.

4. Garnish with green coriander and lemon juice and serve hot with any Indian bread of choice (pp. 104-107).

TOMATO DELIGHT

Serves: 4-5   Preparation time: 20 minutes   Cooking time: 40 minutes

Ingredients

Tomatoes, quartered *1 kg*
Oil *100 ml / ½ cup*
Ginger *(adrak)* paste (p. 8) *7 ½ gm / 1 ½ tsp*
Garlic *(lasan)* paste (p. 8) *10 gm / 1 tsp*
Red chilli powder *10 gm / 1 tsp*
Coriander *(dhaniya)* powder *8 gm / ½ tsp*
Cumin (*jeera*) powder *10 gm / 2 tsp*
Salt to taste
Onion seeds (*kalonji*) *2 gm / ½ tsp*
Fenugreek (*methi*) seeds *1½ gm / ½ tsp*
Mustard (*rai*) seeds *1 ½ gm / ½ tsp*
Whole red chillies *3*
Cherry tomatoes, blanched *20*

Method

1. Heat half the oil in a thick-bottomed wok *(kadhai)*.
2. Add ginger and garlic pastes. Stir-fry for a minute.
3. Add red chilli powder, coriander powder, cumin powder and salt to taste. Add tomatoes and stir-fry till they are cooked.
4. Strain and keep aside.
5. Heat remaining oil. Add onion seeds, fenugreek seeds, mustard seeds and whole red chillies. Let them crackle and then add to the strained sauce.
6. Add cherry tomatoes to the sauce and simmer for about 4 minutes. Serve immediately.

ROGANI MUSHROOMS

(Mushrooms cooked in a rich onion and tomato curry)

Serves: 4   Preparation time: 40 minutes   Cooking time: 30 minutes

Ingredients

Mushrooms *(guchi)*, without stems, boiled *600 gm / 3 cups*
Oil *100 ml / ½ cup*
Bayleaves *(tej patta) 4*
Mace *(javitri) 2 gm / 1/3 tsp*
Cloves *(laung) 4*
Green cardamoms *(choti elaichi) 4*
Black cardamoms *(bari elaichi) 4*
Cinnamon *(dalchini)* sticks, small *2*
Ginger-garlic *(adrak-lasan)* paste (p. 8) *20 gm / 4 tsp*
Tomato purée (p. 8) *300 gm / 1 ½ cups*
Salt to taste
Red chilli powder *10 gm / 2 tsp*
Turmeric *(haldi)* powder *5 gm / 1 tsp*
Coriander (*dhaniya*) powder *10 gm / 2 tsp*
Brown onion paste (p. 6) *150 gm / ¾ cup*
Yoghurt (*dahi*) (p. 6), whisked *50 gm / 3 1/3 tbsp*
Water *100 ml / ½ cup*
Garam masala (p. 6) *a pinch*
Green coriander (*hara dhaniya*), chopped *5 gm / 1 tsp*
Ginger (*adrak*), julienned (long, thin strips) *5 gm / 1 tsp*
Green chillies, julienned (long, thin strips) *5 gm / 1 tsp*

Method

1. Heat oil in a pot (*handi*); add bayleaves, mace, cloves, green cardamoms, black cardamoms and cinnamon. Sauté till they crackle.

2. Stir in ginger-garlic paste dissolved in a little water and stir-fry till the water dries out.

3. Add tomato purée, salt, red chilli powder, turmeric powder, coriander powder; sauté for 2-3 minutes till the oil separates.
4. Add the brown onion paste and yoghurt, stir-fry for 2-3 minutes. Add the mushrooms along with water. Cook on low heat until the curry thickens and the mushrooms are cooked. Remove from heat and transfer to a serving dish.
5. Serve hot, garnished with garam masala, green coriander, julienned ginger and green chillies.

Power-Packed Chilli Powder

To retain the freshness of red chilli powder for a long time, keep a piece of asafoetida in the container.

MINCED PEAS AND POTATOES

Serves: 4-6   Preparation time: 10 minutes   Cooking time: 30 minutes

Ingredients

Peas *(mattar)*, minced *300 gm / 1 ½ cups*
Potatoes (small), diced *5-6*
Green chillies, chopped *1-2*
Ginger *(adrak)*, peeled, chopped (½" piece) *1*
Tomatoes, chopped *400 gm / 2 cups*
Clarified butter *(ghee) 100 ml / ½ cup*
Cumin *(jeera)* seeds *5 gm / 1 ½ tsp*
Cloves *(laung)*, ground *6*
Cinnamon *(dalchini)* sticks, ground *2*
Peppercorns *(kali mirch)*, ground *6-8*
Coriander *(dhaniya)* powder *15 gm / 1 tbsp*
Turmeric *(haldi)* powder *5 gm / 1 tsp*
Red chilli powder *3 gm / ½ tsp*
Salt to taste
Green coriander *(hara dhaniya)*, fresh *30 gm / 2 tbsp*
Garam masala (p. 6) *15 gm / 1 tbsp*

Method

1. Purée the green chillies, ginger and tomatoes.
2. Heat 4 tbsp clarified butter in a wok *(kadhai)* and brown the minced peas till the oil separates. Set aside.
3. Heat 1 tbsp clarified butter. Add the cumin seeds and fry for a few seconds. Add the browned pea paste, ground whole spices, coriander, turmeric and red chilli powder; cook for a few minutes.
4. Stir in the green chillies-ginger-tomato purée; bring to a boil.
5. Mix in the potatoes and cook till tender.
6. Season with salt and garam masala. Garnish with chopped coriander and serve hot.

MATTAR PANEER

(Pea and cottage cheese curry)

Serves: 4-5   Preparation time: 15 minutes   Cooking time: 30 minutes

Ingredients

Cottage cheese *(paneer)* (p. 8), cut into 1 cm cubes *250 gm / 1 ¼ cups*
Green peas *(mattar)*, fresh or frozen *400 gm / 2 cups*
Oil *60 ml / 4 tbsp*
Caraway seeds *(shahi jeera) 3 gm / ⅔ tsp*
Green cardamoms *(choti elaichi) 6*
Cloves *(laung) 6*
Cinnamon *(dalchini)* sticks *2*
Onions, grated *120 gm / ⅔ cup*
Ginger *(adrak)* paste (p. 8) *30 gm / 6 tsp*
Garlic *(lasan)* paste (p. 8) *30 gm / 6 tsp*
Green chilli paste (p. 6) *25 gm / 5 tsp*
White pepper *(safed mirch)* powder *3 gm / ⅔ tsp*
Salt to taste
Garam masala (p. 6) *10 gm / 2 tsp*
Cashewnut *(kaju)* paste *100 gm / ½ cup*
Yoghurt *(dahi)* (p. 6), whisked *200 gm / 1 cup*
Cream *80 gm / 5 ⅓ tbsp*
Green coriander *(hara dhaniya)*, chopped *15 gm / 3 tsp*
Ginger *(adrak)* juliennes (long thin strips) *5 gm / 1 tsp*
Green cardamom (*choti elaichi*) powder *3 gm / ⅔ tsp*

Method

1. Heat the oil in a saucepan and lightly sauté the cottage cheese cubes, a few at a time, till golden. Keep aside.

2. To the remaining oil, add the caraway seeds, green cardamoms, cloves and cinnamon; sauté till they crackle. Add the grated onions, ginger, garlic and green chilli pastes, pepper, salt and garam masala. Sauté for 4-5 minutes.

3. Add the cashewnut paste and yoghurt and cook for 5-6 minutes. Add the green peas and cook over a low fire, stirring occasionally, until the gravy separates from the oil.

4. Add the fried cottage cheese cubes and cream and simmer for a few minutes.

5. Transfer to a bowl and garnish with green coriander, ginger juliennes and sprinkle with green cardamom powder. (You can substitute cottage cheese with 250 gm mushrooms, which do not need to be previously fried.)

Greening Peas

To retain the colour of peas, add a few drops of vinegar.

TANGY POTATOES

Serves: 4   Preparation time: 15 minutes   Cooking time: 40 minutes

Ingredients

Potatoes *600 gm*
Oil *100 ml / ½ cup*
Onion, chopped *20 gm / 4 tsp*
Cumin *(jeera)*, whole *10 gm / 2 tsp*
Turmeric *(haldi)* powder *3 gm / ½ tsp*
Red chilli powder *5 gm / 1 tsp*
Cumin *(jeera)* powder *10 gm / 2 tsp*
Cashewnut *(kaju)* paste (optional) *30 gm / 2 tbsp*
Cloves (*laung*) powder *3 gm / 1 tsp*
Cinnamon *(dalchini)* powder *1 gm / a pinch*
Salt to paste
Yoghurt *(dahi)* (p. 6) *400 gm / 2 cups*

Method

1. Peel the potatoes and soak in water.

2. Heat 1 tbsp oil in a pan and sauté onion till brown.

3. Heat the remaining oil in a wok *(kadhai)*, sauté cumin seeds till they crackle. Add turmeric, red chilli and cumin powders along with ½ cup water.

4. Mix in all the remaining ingredients and cook for 5 minutes.

5. Add the peeled potatoes to the curry and seal with dough. Cook on low flame *(dum)* for 30-35 minutes.

6. Remove from heat, transfer to a serving dish and serve hot.

ZAFRANI KOFTA CURRY

(An exotic cottage cheese, eggs and saffron curry)

Serves: 4-5 Preparation time: 15 minutes Cooking time: 45 minutes

Ingredients

Cottage cheese *(paneer)* (p. 8), grated *500 gm / 2 ½ cups*
White pepper *(safed mirch)* powder *2 gm / ½ tsp*
Cashewnuts *(kaju)*, chopped *50 gm / ¼ cup*
Eggs *2*
Salt to taste
Clarified butter *(ghee) 100 gm / ½ cup*
Onions, chopped *100 gm / ½ cup*
Garlic *(lasan)* paste (p. 8) *25 gm / 5 tsp*
Ginger *(adrak)* paste (p. 8) *25 gm / 5 tsp*
Red chilli powder *4 gm / ¾ tsp*
Turmeric *(haldi)* powder *3 gm / 2/3 tsp*
Garam masala (p. 6) *3 gm / 2/3 tsp*
Fenugreek *(methi)* powder *2 gm / ½ tsp*
Saffron *(kesar)* (dissolved in 1 tbsp milk) *1 gm / a pinch*
Coriander *(dhaniya)* powder *25 gm / 5 tsp*
Green coriander *(hara dhaniya)*, chopped *5 gm / 1 tsp*
Yoghurt *(dahi)* (p. 6) *100 gm / ½ cup*

Method

1. Mix cottage cheese, white pepper, cashewnuts, eggs and salt to taste.
2. Divide into 16 equal portions and make into balls (*koftas*).

3. Heat the clarified butter in a pan. Deep fry the balls until golden. Remove from the pan.

4. In the remaining butter, add the chopped onions, ginger-garlic pastes, red chilli powder, coriander powder and turmeric powder. Cook for 10 minutes till the mixture turns brown and separates from the butter.

5. Add garam masala, half the fenugreek powder and yoghurt and cook for about 10 minutes.

6. Add the cottage cheese balls very slowly to the gravy and simmer for 5 minutes.

7. Sprinkle the remaining fenugreek powder, saffron dissolved in milk and chopped green coriander. Serve with any Indian bread of choice (pp. 104-107).

Egging Along

Pierce eggs with a sharp pin before boiling, to prevent them from cracking.

BISI BELE HULIYANA

(Spiced sambhar with rice)

Serves: 4   Preparation time: 40 minutes   Cooking time: 40 minutes

Ingredients

Basmati rice *300 gm / 1 ¼ cups*
Red gram *(arhar) 160 gm / ⅔ cup*
Bengal gram *(chana dal)*, husked, split *60 gm / ¼ cup*
Black gram *(dhuli urad dal)*, husked split *30 gm / 2 tbsp*
Cinnamon *(dalchini)* sticks of *1" 2*
Green cardamoms (*choti elaichi*) *5*
Cloves *(laung) 5*
Cumin *(jeera)* seeds *2 ½ gm / 1 tsp*
Fenugreek seeds (*methi dana*) *5 gm / 1 tsp*
Groundnut oil *(moongphali tel)* to deep-fry
Cashewnuts *(kaju)*, split *20 gm / 4 tsp*
Green peas *(mattar) 60 gm / ¼ cup*
Cauliflower *(phool gobi)*, small florets *60 gm / ¼ cup*
Tomatoes, chopped *400 gm / 1 ⅔ cups*
Tamarind *(imli)* extract *45 ml / 3 tbsp*
Asafoetida *(hing) 2 ½ gm / ½ tsp*
Red chilli powder *2 ½ gm / ½ tsp*
Turmeric *(haldi)* powder *5 gm / 1 tsp*
Salt to taste
Curry leaves *(meethi neem ke patte) 10*
Groundnut oil *(moongphali tel)* for tempering *30 ml / 2 tbsp*
Mustard (*rai*) seeds *2 ½ gm / ½ tsp*
Red chillies, whole *2*

Method

1. Wash rice and red gram and soak separately for 30 minutes.

2. To make *sambhar* powder, broil Bengal gram and

black gram separately on a griddle till light brown.

3. Broil cinnamon, cardamoms, cloves, cumin seeds and fenugreek seeds for 30 seconds. Grind together with the broiled Bengal gram and black gram in a blender.

4. Deep fry the cashewnuts till golden brown. Keep aside.

5. Put red gram in a pot *(handi)*, add 2 ½ lt / 10 cups water and bring to a boil. Simmer until almost cooked.

6. Drain rice and add to the cooked gram, along with peas and cauliflower. Simmer for 10 minutes, stirring occasionally.

7. Stir in the tomatoes, tamarind extract and the asafoetida.

8. Add red chilli powder, turmeric and salt. Stir in the blended *sambhar* powder.

9. Cover and simmer till rice and vegetables are cooked and become porridge-like. Sprinkle curry leaves and simmer.

10. Heat 30 ml / 2 tbsp oil in a wok *(kadhai)* and sauté the mustard seeds. Add whole red chillies and stir for 15 seconds.

11. Pour the tempering over the red gram-rice-vegetable mixture. Stir for 2 minutes. Garnish with cashewnuts and serve with pickle and *pappadams*.

BUTTERED VEGETABLES

Serves: 4   Preparation time: 1 hour   Cooking time: 45 minutes

Ingredients

Green beans *(sem) 200 gm*
Carrots *(gajar) 200 gm*
Potatoes *200 gm*
Cauliflower *(phool gobi) 200 gm*
Green peas *(mattar)*, shelled *100 gm / ½ cup*
Red pumpkin *(lal kaddu) 200 gm*
Butter *250 gm / 1 ¼ cups*
Ginger-garlic *(adrak-lasan)* paste (p. 8) *80 gm / 5 ½ tbsp*
Tomatoes, chopped *1 kg*
Salt to taste
Red chilli powder *5 gm / 1 tbsp*
Green chillies, chopped *5*
Cream *150 gm / ¾ cup*
Dry fenugreek (*kasoori methi*) powder *15 gm / 1 tbsp*
Green coriander *(hara dhaniya)*, chopped *25 gm / 5 tsp*

Method

1. Wash, peel and cut vegetables into 1 cm dices.
2. For the curry, melt half the butter in a heavy-bottomed pan. Add ginger-garlic paste, tomatoes, salt, red chilli powder and 2 ½ cups water. Cover and simmer till the tomatoes are mashed.
3. Cool and strain the curry through a fine sieve.
4. In a wok *(kadhai)*, melt the remaining butter. Sauté green chillies over medium heat and add the vegetables. Stir for 4 minutes, pour in the curry and simmer till the vegetables are cooked.
5. Add cream and fenugreek powder along with salt.
6. Serve hot, topped with cream and coriander.

LOTUS STEMS IN AN EXOTIC CURRY

Serves: 4   Preparation time: 10 minutes   Cooking time: 30 minutes

Ingredients

Lotus stems *(kamal kakri) 800 gm*
Mustard oil (*sarson ka tel) 250 ml / 1 ¼ cups*
Water
Cloves *(laung) 2*
Green cardamoms *(choti elaichi) 2*
Fennel *(saunf)* powder *30 gm / 2 tbsp*
Salt *5 gm / 1 tsp*
Cumin *(jeera)* powder *2 gm / ⅓ tsp*
Cinnamon *(dalchini)* powder *3 gm / ½ tsp*
Black cardamom *(bari elaichi)* powder *6 gm / 1 tsp*
Yoghurt (*dahi*) (p. 6), whisked *1 kg / 7 ½ cups*

Method

1. Scrape away the skin of the lotus stems. Cut into 1½" long pieces, discarding the ends. Wash well and drain.
2. Heat the mustard oil in a wok (*kadhai*) and deep fry the lotus stems till they are half cooked. Drain and keep aside.
3. Add the water and the lotus stems to the same wok (*kadhai*) and bring to a boil. Add all the spices and mix in the yoghurt. Stirring regularly, cook till the curry thickens and the lotus stems are tender.
4. Remove into a serving dish and serve hot.

DHINGRI SHABNAM

(A delightful combination of mushroom and cottage cheese dumplings)

Serves: 4-5   Preparation time: 45 minutes   Cooking time: 30 minutes

Ingredients

For the *koftas*:

Cottage cheese *(paneer)* (p. 8) *300 gm*
Flour *(maida) 50 gm / 1/4 cup*
Oil to deep fry *koftas 120 ml / 2/3 cup*

For the filling:

Morels / button mushrooms *(guchi) 20 gm / 4 tsp*
Butter *(makhan) 5 gm / 1 tsp*
Khoya (p. 8) *15 gm / 3 tsp*
Cashewnuts (*kaju*), chopped *8*
Raisins *(kismish) 16*
Green chilli, deseeded, finely chopped *1*
Green coriander *(hara dhaniya)*, finely chopped *10 gm / 2 tsp*
Cottage cheese *(paneer)* (p. 8) *20 gm / 4 tsp*

For the gravy:

Oil *60 ml / 4 tbsp*
Fenugreek seeds *(methi dana) 1 gm / 1/4 tsp*
Onions, chopped *50 gm / 1/4 cup*
Garlic *(lasan)* paste (p. 8) *10 gm / 2 tsp*
Ginger *(adrak)* paste (p. 8) *10 gm / 2 tsp*
Turmeric *(haldi)* powder *2 gm / 1/4 tsp*
Red chilli powder *a pinch*
Salt to taste
Cashewnut *(kaju)* paste *40 gm / 2 2/3 tbsp*
Yoghurt *(dahi)* (p. 6) *75 gm / 1/3 cup*
Onion paste (p. 8), fried *20 gm / 4 tsp*
Garam masala (p. 6) *2 gm / 1/4 tsp*

Method

1. For the *koftas*, mash 200 gm / 1 cup cottage cheese in a bowl. Add flour and mix to make a dough. Divide into 8 equal portions and shape into balls.

2. For the filling, soak the morels / mushrooms in lukewarm water for 5 minutes. Drain, wash in running water for 2-3 minutes and then soak until they become soft and swollen. Drain, squeeze out the excess water, remove stems and slice thin.

3. Melt the butter in a pan, add the morels / mushrooms and sauté over medium heat for 30 seconds.

4. Add the *khoya* and fry over medium heat until light golden. Add the chopped cashewnuts and raisins.

5. Mash the remaining cottage cheese in a bowl. Add the morels / mushrooms, *khoya* and the remaining ingredients. Mix well. Divide into 8 equal portions.

6. Flatten the *kofta* balls; place a portion of the filling in the middle of each and roll into balls again.

7. Heat oil in a wok *(kadhai)* and deep fry the *koftas* until light golden. Remove and keep aside.

8. For the gravy, heat the oil in a wok *(kadhai)*. Add fenugreek seeds and sauté over medium heat until they begin to crackle.

9. Add chopped onions and sauté until light golden. Add the ginger-garlic paste, and fry for a minute. Stir in turmeric, red chilli powder and salt.

10. Add the cashewnut paste and yoghurt and cook until the oil separates from the gravy.

11. Stir in the fried onion paste. Add 4 ½ cups water, bring to a boil and then simmer until the gravy becomes sauce-like.

12. Remove and strain the gravy into another pan. Return the strained gravy to heat, gently add the *koftas* and simmer for 5 minutes.

13. Sprinkle with garam masala and stir. Transfer to a bowl and serve with *pulao* or any Indian bread of choice (pp. 104-107).

Salty Solution

Add a pinch of salt while frying dumplings and you will consume less oil.

CASHEWNUT AND MUSHROOM CURRY

Serves: 4   Preparation time: 45 minutes   Cooking time: 25 minutes

Ingredients

Cashewnuts *(kaju) 200 gm / 1 cup*
Mushrooms *(guchi) 750 gm / 3 ¾ cups*
Butter *(makhan) 60 gm / 5 tbsp*
Cloves *(laung) 10*
Mace *(javitri) 3 gm / 1 tsp*
Cumin *(jeera)* seeds *4 gm / 1 tsp*
Ginger *(adrak)* paste (p. 8) *20 gm / 4 tsp*
Garlic *(lasan)* paste (p. 8) *10 gm / 2 tsp*
Onions, browned *150 gm / 2 cups*
Tomato paste *45 gm / 3 tbsp*
Coriander *(dhaniya)* powder *3 gm / 1 tsp*
Turmeric *(haldi)* powder *2 gm / ½ tsp*
Red chilli powder *3 gm / 1 tsp*
Salt to taste
Cream *60 gm / 5 tbsp*
Green coriander *(hara dhaniya) 15 gm / 1 tbsp*

Method

1. Soak cashewnuts in warm water for half an hour. Drain and keep aside. Wash the mushrooms.

2. Heat butter in a thick-bottomed pan. Add cloves, mace and cumin seeds and fry till the cumin seeds begin to crackle.

3. Stir ginger and garlic pastes and stir-fry for a minute. Add the browned onions and tomato paste along with coriander, turmeric and red chilli powders. Stir-fry till the butter appears on the surface.

4. Add 2 cups of water and salt; bring to boil and simmer for 15 minutes.

5. Add mushrooms and cashewnuts and simmer for another 3 minutes. Top with cream.

6. Serve hot, garnished with chopped green coriander.

PANEER BIRBALI

(Cottage cheese curried in tomatoes and garnished with cream)

Serves: 4-5   Preparation time: 10 minutes   Cooking time: 20 minutes

Ingredients

Cottage cheese *(paneer)* (p. 8), block *1 kg*
Oil *200 ml / 1 cup*
Green cardamoms (*choti elaichi*) *3 gm / 2/3 tsp*
Bayleaves (*tej patta*) *2*
Cumin (*jeera*) seeds *3 gm / 2/3 tsp*
Cinnamon *(dalchini)* sticks *3*
Ginger (*adrak*) paste (p. 8) *40 gm / 2 2/3 tbsp*
Garlic (*lasan*) paste (p. 8) *40 gm / 2 2/3 tbsp*
Red chilli powder *10 gm / 2 tsp*
Onions, chopped *100 gm / ½ cup*
Tomatoes, chopped *300 gm / 1 ½ cups*
Mace (*javitri*) powder *3 gm / 2/3 tsp*
Salt to taste
Cream *6 gm / 1 1/3 tsp*
Gram flour (*besan*) or maize flour (*makkai ka atta*) *150 gm / ¾ cup*
Milk *50 ml / 3 1/3 tbsp*
Green coriander (*hara dhaniya*), chopped *15 gm / 3 tsp*
Ginger (*adrak*), julienned (long, thin strips) *6 gm / 1 1/3 tsp*
Cashewnuts (*kaju*) *100 gm / ½ cup*

Method

1. Heat 80 ml / 1/3 cup oil in a pan. Add cardamoms, bayleaves, cumin seeds and cinnamon sticks; sauté over medium heat for 30 seconds.
2. Add the ginger and garlic pastes, red chilli powder and onions; sauté for 5 minutes. Add the tomatoes

and 1 ½ cups of water. Cover and cook over medium heat for 5-10 minutes. Uncover, stir and cook for another 5 minutes, or until the oil separates from the gravy.

3. Add mace, salt and three-fourths of the cream. Strain the gravy and keep aside.

4. Mix the gram flour in milk to make a thick batter. Beat the batter for 3 minutes. Coat the cottage cheese block with the batter. Heat the remaining oil in a pan and shallow fry until light brown.

5. Slice the cottage cheese lengthwise. Place on a platter and pour the hot sauce over it. Garnish with chopped coriander leaves and ginger juliennes. Sprinkle with crushed cashewnuts.

Fresh and Fresher

Cottage cheese will remain fresh for longer if you keep it in a container filled with water in the fridge.

DAL PANCHMELA

(Five-in-one pulse delight)

Serves: 4 Preparation time: 15 minutes Cooking time: 1 hour

Ingredients

Lentils *(masoor dal) 45 gm / 3 tbsp*
Bengal gram *(chana dal)* *45 gm / 3 tbsp*
Black gram, split *(dhuli urad dal)* *45 gm / 3 tbsp*
Red gram *(arhar dal) 45 gm / 3 tbsp*
Green gram, split *(dhuli moong dal)* *45 gm / 3 tbsp*
Water as required
Salt *10 gm / 2 tsp*
Turmeric *(haldi)* powder *5 gm / 1 tsp*
Red chilli powder *5 gm / 1 tsp*
Oil *30 ml / 2 tbsp*
Butter *15 gm / 1 tbsp*
Cumin *(jeera)* seeds *5 gm / 1 tsp*
Ginger *(adrak)*, chopped *10 gm / 2 tsp*
Tomatoes, chopped *60 gm / 4 tbsp*
Green coriander *(hara dhaniya)*, chopped *5 gm / 1 tsp*

Method

1. Pick, clean and wash all the pulses.
2. Put the pulses along with water, salt, turmeric powder and red chilli powder in a pot *(handi)* and cook on low heat for 40-45 minutes till they are tender.
3. Remove from heat and keep aside.
4. Heat oil and butter in a pan. Add cumin seeds and sauté till they crackle. Add ginger and stir-fry to a light brown colour.
5. Put in the tomatoes and sauté for a minute. Stir in the green coriander and remove from heat.
6. Temper the cooked pulses with this mixture and serve hot.

PICKLED LAMB CURRY

Serves: 4-5   *Preparation time: 2 hours 30 minutes*   *Cooking time: 30 minutes*

Ingredients

Lamb chops *8*
Raw papaya *(kacha papita)*, pounded *a small piece*
Ginger-garlic *(adrak-lasan)* paste (p. 8) *20 gm / 4 tsp*
Salt to taste
Gram flour *(besan) 10 gm / 2 tsp*
Aniseed *(saunf) 5 gm / 1 tsp*
Black cardamoms *(bari elaichi) 3 gm / ½ tsp*
Black pepper *(kali mirch) 5 gm / 1 tsp*
Cloves *(laung) 3 gm / ½ tsp*
Meat tenderizer 5 gm / 1 tsp
Mustard oil *(sarson ka tel) 50 ml / ¼ cup*
Chaat masala *5 gm / 1 tsp*
Mustard *(rai)* seeds *5 gm / 1 tsp*
Onion seeds *(kalonji) 5 gm / 1 tsp*
Lemon juice *15 ml / 1 tbsp*
Red chilli powder *15 gm / 1 tbsp*
Yoghurt *(dahi)* (p. 6), whisked *50 gm / ¼ cup*

Method

1. Flatten the chops with a steak hammer. Rub with papaya, ginger-garlic paste, salt and keep aside.
2. Stir the gram flour in a pan till light brown and sprinkle over the lamb chops.
3. Add the remaining ingredients, except chaat masala and lemon juice, to the yoghurt and mix well. Marinate the chops in this mixture for 2 hours.
4. Preheat the oven to 175 °C / 350 °F.
5. Skewer the chops and roast in a hot tandoor or oven until cooked, basting occasionally.
6. Remove the chops from the skewer. Sprinkle chaat masala and lemon juice and serve hot.

ROGAN JOSH

(Meat cooked in yoghurt and whole spices)

Serves: 4   Preparation time: 30 minutes   Cooking time: 1 hour

Ingredients

Lamb shoulder, cut into cubes *1 kg*
Clarified butter (*ghee*) *150 gm / ¾ cup*
Asafoetida (*hing*) powder *a pinch*
Green cardamoms (*choti elaichi*) *10*
Cinnamon (*dalchini*) sticks *3*
Cloves (*laung*) *5*
Onions, sliced *450 gm / 2 ¼ cups*
Ginger *(adrak)*, chopped
75 gm / 5 tbsp
Garlic *(lasan)*, chopped *45 gm / 3 tbsp*
Yoghurt *(dahi)* (p. 6), whisked
600 gm / 3 cups
Deghi mirch powder *15 gm / 1 tbsp*
Salt to taste
Water *500 ml / 2 ½ cups*

Method

1. Heat clarified butter in a wok *(kadhai)*. Add asafoetida, green cardamoms, cinnamon sticks and cloves. Sauté till they crackle.

2. Add onions and stir-fry till golden brown.

3. Stir in ginger and garlic and sauté for 2 minutes. Add the lamb cubes and stir-fry for 15 minutes.

4. Add the remaining ingredients except water. Cover and cook on low heat for 30 minutes.

5. Increase heat and stir-fry till the oil separates.

6. Stir in water and cook till the lamb cubes are tender. Remove from heat and serve hot.

NILGIRI KORMA

(Lamb cooked in coconut curry)

Serves: 4-5   Preparation time: 15 minutes   Cooking time: 1 hour

Ingredients

Lamb cubes, boneless *1 kg*
Red chillies *20*
Coriander *(dhaniya)* seeds *50 gm / 3 1/3 tbsp*
Cumin *(jeera)* seeds *15 gm / 3 tsp*
Fennel *(saunf)* seeds *10 gm / 2 tsp*
Poppy seeds *(khus khus) 10 gm / 2 tsp*
Refined oil *100 ml / ½ cup*
Cinnamon *(dalchini)* sticks *5*
Cloves *(laung) 8*
Green cardamoms *(choti elaichi) 8*
Bayleaf *(tej patta) 1*
Onion paste (p. 8) *200 gm / 1 cup*
Garlic *(lasan)* paste (p. 8) *40 gm / 2 2/3 tbsp*
Ginger *(adrak)* paste *40 gm / 2 2/3 tbsp*
Salt to taste
Fresh coconut *(nariyal)*, grated *500 gm / 2 ½ cups*
Green coriander *(hara dhaniya)*, chopped *20 gm / 4 tsp*
Fresh mint *(pudina)*, chopped *20 gm / 4 tsp*

Method

1. Dry roast red chillies, coriander, cumin, fennel and poppy seeds; grind to a fine paste using 50-60 ml of water.
2. Heat the oil in a pan, add the cinnamon sticks, cloves, cardamoms and bayleaf. Sauté over medium heat until they begin to crackle. Add the onion and garlic-ginger pastes and cook for 5-6 minutes.
3. In a separate pan, heat 2 cups of water, add the

lamb cubes, bring to a slow boil and cook for 10 minutes.

4. Add the boiled lamb cubes and salt to the sautéd spices. Cook over medium heat for 10-15 minutes, stirring constantly.

5. Add a cup of hot water, cover and cook on low heat until the lamb is almost cooked.

6. Grind the grated coconut in a liquidizer to a very fine paste. Add 150 ml hot water to the coconut paste and strain through a fine cheesecloth to get thick, fresh coconut milk.

7. Add the coconut milk to the lamb, uncover and cook for 10 minutes until the gravy thickens.

8. Serve hot, garnished with chopped green coriander and mint.

Freeze for Freshness

Fresh coconuts tend to get spoiled, even in the refrigerator. Keep them in the freezer and they will remain fresh even for a month.

GOSHT SHAHI KORMA

(Lamb curried with yoghurt, dried milk, cream and almonds)

Serves: 4-5   Preparation time: 1 hour   Cooking time: 30 minutes

Ingredients

Lamb, boneless *1 kg*
Ginger (*adrak*) paste (p. 8) *25 gm / 5 tsp*
Garlic (*lasan*) paste (p. 8) *25 gm / 5 tsp*
Clarified butter (*ghee*) *150 gm / ¾ cup*
White butter (*safed makhan*) *100 gm / ½ cup*
Bayleaves (*tej patta*) *2*
Cinnamon (*dalchini*) sticks *5*
Green cardamom (*choti elaichi*) powder *2 gm / ½ tsp*
Onions, sliced *150 gm / ¾ cup*
Yoghurt (*dahi*) (p. 6) *250 gm / 1 ¼ cups*
Almond (*badam*) paste *50 gm / ¼ cup*
Cream *100 gm / ½ cup*
Green chillies *6-10*
White pepper (*safed mirch*) powder *2 gm / ½ tsp*
Salt to taste
Green cardamoms (*choti elaichi*) *10*
Khoya (p. 8) *50 gm / ¼ cup*
Silver leaf (*varq*) *2*

Method

1. Wash and pat dry the lamb; cut into small cubes.
2. Rub the ginger and garlic pastes on the lamb cubes and keep aside for 1 hour.
3. Heat the clarified butter and white butter. Add bayleaves, cinnamon sticks and cardamoms; sauté till

they crackle. Then add the onions and sauté till soft.

4. Add the cubed lamb and cook over high heat until the lamb changes colour.

5. Add the yoghurt and almond paste and cook on low heat for another 25 minutes, or until the lamb cubes are tender. Season with cream, green chillies, white pepper powder, salt and green cardamom powder.

6. Serve, garnished with grated *khoya* and silver leaves, accompanied by any bread of choice (pp. 104-107).

Silver(y) Curd!

If you run out of the curd needed to set fresh curd, put a silver coin in warm milk. You will get thick curd. (Don't forget to remove the silver coin!)

RAJASTHANI MEAT

Serves: 4-5   Preparation time: 15 minutes   Cooking time: 45 minutes

Ingredients

Lamb, boneless, cut into 3 cm cubes *1½ kg*

Yoghurt *(dahi)* (p. 6), whisked *250 gm / 1 ¼ cups*

White pepper (*safed mirch*) powder *5 gm / 1 tsp*

Almonds (*badam*), blanched *60 gm / ⅓ cup*

Coconut (*nariyal*) pieces *50 gm / ¼ cup*

Oil *150 gm / ¾ cup*, Salt to taste

Ginger (*adrak*) juliennes (long, thin strips) *20 gm / 4 tsp*

Green cardamom (*choti elaichi*) powder *3 gm / ⅔ tsp*

Cream *120 gm / ⅔ cup*

Lemon juice *10 ml / 2 tsp*

Rose water (*gulab jal*) *5 ml / 1 tsp*

Green chillies, chopped *6*

Method

1. Clean the lamb and boil for 5 minutes in a pan with salt and 7½ cups of water. Drain and wash the lamb.

2. Mix yoghurt and white pepper and keep aside.

3. Blend almonds and coconut with ¼ cup water to a fine paste.

4. Heat the oil in a pan, add the blanched lamb, spiced yoghurt, ginger and salt. Add 800 ml / 4 cups water, cover and simmer, stirring occasionally, until lamb is tender and the liquid has almost evaporated.

5. Add the almond and coconut paste and stir for 2 minutes. Sprinkle cardamom powder and stir.

6. Stir in cream, lemon juice and rose water. Sprinkle green chillies. Seal the pan with dough and bake in a preheated oven at 135°C / 270 °F for 15 minutes.

7. Break the seal and transfer the cooked lamb to a shallow dish.

DUM SHAHI KOFTAS

(An exotic meat-ball curry with the added richness of dried apricots)

Serves: 4-5   Preparation time: 25 minutes   Cooking time: 30 minutes

Ingredients

For the *koftas*:

Lamb (very finely minced) *1 kg*
Butter *(makhan) 50 gm / 3 1/3 tbsp*
Coriander *(dhaniya)* powder *4 gm / 3/4 tsp*
Fennel *(saunf)* powder *4 gm / 3/4 tsp*
Garlic *(lasan)* paste (p. 8) *25 gm / 5 tsp*
Ginger *(adrak)* paste (p. 8) *25 gm / 5 tsp*
Green chillies, finely chopped *6 gm / 1 tsp*
Green coriander *(hara dhaniya)*, finely chopped *10 gm / 2 tsp*
Onions, grated *120 gm / 2/3 cup*
Salt for seasoning
White pepper *(safed mirch)* powder *4 gm / 3/4 tsp*
Dried apricots *(anjeer)*, diced *150 gm / 3/4 cup*

For the gravy:

Oil *80 ml / 1/3 cup*
Bayleaves *(tej patta) 2*
Cloves *(laung) 10*
Green cardamoms *(choti elaichi) 10*
Cinnamon *(dalchini)* sticks *3*
Onion paste (p. 8) *160 gm / 3/4 cup*
Ginger *(adrak)* paste (p. 8) *50 gm / 3 1/3 tbsp*
Garlic *(lasan)* paste (p. 8) *50 gm / 3 1/3 tbsp*
Red chilli powder *10 gm / 2 tsp*
Tomatoes, skinned, deseeded, chopped *350 gm / 1 3/4 cups*
Salt for seasoning
Cream *10 gm / 2 tsp*

Garam masala (p. 6) *10 gm / 2 tsp*
Green coriander *(hara dhaniya)*, chopped *15 gm / 3 tsp*
Mace *(javitri)* powder *4 gm / ¾ tsp*
Saffron *(kesar)*, dissolved in 15 ml milk *1 gm / a pinch*
Vetivier *(kewda) 3 drops*

Method

1. Mix all the ingredients for the *koftas*—except for the diced apricots—with the lamb mince, using a wooden spoon. Mix thoroughly until the mixture sticks to the spoon. Season with salt to taste. Divide this mixture into 25 balls.

2. Stuff each meat ball with a portion of the diced apricots.

3. Heat the oil in a pan. Add the bay leaves, cloves, cardamoms and cinnamon sticks; sauté over medium heat for 30 seconds.

4. Add the onion paste, ginger and garlic pastes; sauté for 30 seconds. Add red chilli powder and salt. Stir and cook for 3-4 minutes. Add the chopped tomatoes and simmer over medium heat until the oil separates from the tomato gravy.

5. Gently slip in the *koftas*, add 1 ½ cups hot water and sprinkle garam masala. Cover the pan and simmer for 10 minutes.

6. Add cream, saffron mixture, mace powder and vetivier. Remove from heat.

7. Garnish with green coriander and serve hot with rice or any Indian bread of choice (pp. 104-107).

ANAR-I-GOSHT

(Lamb marinated in pomegranate juice)

Serves: 4-5   Preparation time: 6-12 hours   Cooking time: 45 minutes

Ingredients

Lamb, cubed *1 kg*
Pomegranate (*anar*) juice *250 ml / 1 ¼ cups*
Oil *100 ml / ½ cup*
Bayleaves (*tej patta*) *3*
Cloves (*laung*) *10*
Cinnamon (*dalchini*) sticks *5*
Green cardamoms (*choti elaichi*) *10*
Onions, chopped / sliced *200 gm / 1 cup*
Ginger (*adrak*) paste (p. 8) *60 gm / 4 tbsp*
Garlic (*lasan*) paste (p. 8) *60 gm / 4 tbsp*
Red chilli powder *10 gm / 2 tsp*
Yoghurt (*dahi*) (p. 6) *200 gm / 1 cup*
Garam masala (p. 6) *2 gm / ½ tsp*
Coriander (*dhaniya*) powder *10 gm / 2 tsp*
Cumin (*jeera*) powder *6 gm / 1 ⅓ tsp*
Mace (*javitri*) powder *3 gm / ⅔ tsp*
Nutmeg (*jaiphal*) powder *2 gm / ½ tsp*
Salt to taste
Black pepper (*kali mirch*), crushed *10 gm / 2 tsp*
Saffron (*kesar*) *a pinch*
Milk *30 ml / 2 tbsp*
Almonds (*badam*), fried *250 gm / 1 ¼ cups*
Mint (*pudina*) leaves, chopped *8 gm / 1 ⅔ tsp*

Method

1. Marinate the lamb cubes in pomegranate juice for 6-12 hours.

2. Heat the oil in a pan; add the whole spices and

sauté over medium heat until they crackle.

3. Add the onions, sauté until soft and golden in colour. Add ginger and garlic pastes and red chili powder. Stir and cook for 5 minutes.

4. Add the marinated lamb with the marinade, stir and cook for 10-15 minutes over medium heat until a pleasant aroma emanates.

5. Add the yoghurt, stir and cook for 5 minutes. Reduce heat and cook until the lamb is tender.

6. Sprinkle garam masala, coriander, cumin, mace and nutmeg powders, salt and crushed black pepper.

7. Transfer to a serving dish, sprinkle with saffron dissolved in milk, fried almonds and mint leaves.

Almond Power!

To preserve almonds and other dry fruits, add a couple of cloves to their containers.

LAMB WITH SPINACH

Serves: 4   Preparation time: 1 hour   Cooking time: 45 minutes

Ingredients

Lamb, cut into boneless cubes *800 gm*
Green coriander *(hara dhaniya)*, chopped *200 gm / 1 cup*
Mint *(pudina)*, fresh *100 gm / ½ cup*
Spinach *(palak)*, chopped *300 gm / 1 ½ cups*
Poppy seeds (*khus khus*) *20 gm / 4 tsp*
Cashewnuts *(kaju) 80 gm / ½ cup*
Oil *100 ml / ½ cup*
Green cardamoms (*choti elaichi*) *8*
Cloves (*laung*) *6*
Onion paste (p. 8) *100 gm / ½ cup*
Ginger-garlic *(adrak-lasan)* paste (p. 8) *40 gm / ⅔ tbsp*
Tomatoes, chopped *125 gm / ½ cup*
Yellow chilli powder *15 gm / 1 tbsp*
Peppercorns *(kali mirch) 10*
Salt to taste
Cream *50 gm / ¼ cup*

Method

1. Wash the coriander, mint and spinach. Blanch spinach in salted water for one and a half minutes. Cool. Blend with mint and coriander. Keep aside.

2. Soak the poppy seeds and cashewnuts in hot water for 30 minutes. Blend to make a fine paste.

3. Heat oil in a heavy-bottomed pan. Sauté cardamoms and cloves till they crackle.

4. Add onion and ginger-garlic paste and stir-fry for 5-6 minutes. Add lamb cubes and stir-fry till they are evenly coated.

5. Add tomatoes, yellow chilli powder, peppercorns and salt. Stir-fry for 2 minutes. Add 1 cup water, bring to a boil; then simmer till the water evaporates.

6. Add the poppy seed-cashewnut paste and the blended purée. Simmer till the lamb is cooked.

7. Drizzle cream on top and serve hot.

LAMB-DO-PIAZA

(Lamb curry with lots of onions)

Serves: 4-5   Preparation time: 15 minutes   Cooking time: 45 minutes

Ingredients

Lamb, cubed *1 kg*
Button onions *300 gm / 1 ½ cups*
Butter *(makhan) 20 gm / 1 1/3 tbsp*
Refined oil *100 ml / 1 cup*
Turmeric *(haldi)* powder *5 gm / 1 tsp*
Bayleaves (*tej patta*) *3*
Cloves *(laung) 10*
Cinnamon *(dalchini)* sticks *5*
Red chillies, whole *8*
Green cardamoms *(choti elaichi) 10*
Onions, chopped / sliced *200 gm / 1 cup*
Ginger *(adrak)* paste (p. 8) *60 gm / 4 tbsp*
Garlic *(lasan)* paste (p. 8) *60 gm / 4 tbsp*
Tomatoes, skinned, deseeded, chopped *300 gm / 1 ½ cups*
Garam masala (p. 6) *12 gm / 2 ½ tsp*
Coriander *(dhaniya)* powder *10 gm / 2 tsp*
Cumin *(jeera)* powder *6 gm / 1 1/3 tsp*
Mace *(javitri)* powder *3 gm / 2/3 tsp*
Nutmeg *(jaiphal)*, powdered *½*
Black pepper *(kali mirch)*, crushed *10 gm / 2 tsp*
Salt to taste
Green coriander *(hara dhaniya)*, chopped *5 gm / 1 tsp*
Ginger *(adrak)* juliennes (long, thin strips) *5 gm / 1 tsp*

Method

1. Blanch the button onions and toss in hot butter for a few minutes.
2. Heat the oil in a pan, add the turmeric and the whole spices and sauté over medium heat until they begin to crackle.

3. Add the onions and sauté until soft and golden in colour. Add the ginger and garlic pastes and chopped tomatoes. Stir and cook for 5 minutes.

4. Add the lamb, stir and cook for 10-15 minutes over medium heat until a pleasant aroma emanates. Reduce heat and simmer on low fire until the lamb is tender.

5. Sprinkle with garam masala, coriander, cumin, mace and nutmeg powders and crushed black pepper. Add salt to taste. Add the button onions and stir. Cover and cook for 2-3 minutes.

6. Serve hot, garnished with green coriander and ginger juliennes.

Betel-Nut at Work!

Lamb will become tender and cook fast if betel-nut pieces are added to it while cooking.

KHADA MASALA GOSHT

(Lamb with whole spices)

Serves: 4-5   Preparation time: 15 minutes   Cooking time: 45 minutes

Ingredients

Lamb, cubed *1 kg*
Oil *100 ml / ½ cup*
Bayleaves *(tej patta) 3*
Cloves *(laung) 10*
Cinnamon *(dalchini)* sticks *5*
Red chillies, whole *8*
Green cardamoms *(choti elaichi) 10*
Onions, chopped / sliced
200 gm / 1 cup
Ginger *(adrak)* paste (p. 8)
60 gm / 4 tbsp
Garlic *(lasan)* paste (p. 8)
60 gm / 4 tbsp
Garam masala (p. 6) *2 gm / ½ tsp*
Coriander *(dhaniya)* powder
10 gm / 2 tsp
Cumin *(jeera)* powder *6 gm / 1 1/3 tsp*
Salt to taste
Mace *(javitri)* powder *3 gm / 2/3 tsp*
Nutmeg *(jaiphal)*, powdered *½*
Black pepper *(kali mirch)*, crushed
10 gm / 2 tsp
Green chillies, whole *12*
Fresh mint *(pudina)* chopped *8 gm / 1 2/3 tsp*
Yoghurt *(dahi)* (p. 6), whisked *200 gm / 1 cup*

Method

1. Heat the oil in a pan. Add the whole spices and sauté over medium heat until they begin to crackle.
2. Add the onions and sauté until soft and golden in colour. Add the ginger and garlic pastes, stir and cook for 5 minutes.

3. Add the lamb cubes and cook for 10-15 minutes over medium heat until the lamb emits a pleasant aroma.
4. Add yoghurt, stir and cook for 5 minutes. Reduce heat and cook until the lamb is tender.
5. Sprinkle with garam masala, coriander powder, cumin powder, salt, mace powder, nutmeg powder and the crushed black pepper.
6. Arrange the green chillies over the cooked meat and cover the pan. Cook for 2-3 minutes.
7. Serve, garnished with fresh mint leaves.

Meat(y) Treat

Leftover meat makes 'great' stuffing for paranthas. Add chopped onions and coriander leaves for an extra flavour.

GOSHT GULFAM

(Lamb with cottage cheese)

Serves: 4-5   Preparation time: 15 minutes   Cooking time: 1 hour

Ingredients

Lamb (shoulder / leg) *1 kg*
Cottage cheese *(paneer)* (p. 8), grated *100 gm / ½ cup*
Almonds *(badam) 25 gm / 5 tsp*
Pistachios *(pista)*, blanched, halved *50 gm / ¼ cup*
Morels *(guchi) 20 gm / 4 tsp*
Salt to taste
White pepper *(safed mirch)* powder *10 gm / 2 tsp*
Red chilli powder *12 gm / 2 ½ tsp*
Garam masala (p. 6) *10 gm / 2 tsp*
Ginger *(adak)* paste (p. 8) *40 gm / 2 ⅔ tbsp*
Garlic *(lasan)* paste (p. 8) *40 gm / 2 ⅔ tbsp*
Cream *30 gm / 2 tbsp*
Oil *80 ml / 5 ⅓ tbsp*
Bayleaves *(tej patta) 2*
Green cardamom *(choti elaichi)* powder *5 gm / 1 tsp*
Cinnamon *(dalchini)* powder *5 gm / 1 tsp*
Water / chicken stock *300-400 ml / 1 ½-2 cups*
Onion paste (p. 8) *100 gm / ½ cup*
Tomatoes, diced *100 gm / ½ cup*
Mace *(javitri)* powder *3 gm / ⅔ tsp*
Green chillies, slit *10 gm / 2 tsp*
Cumin *(jeera)* powder *10 gm / 2 tsp*
Green coriander *(hara dhaniya)*, chopped *15 gm / 3 tsp*

Method

1. Debone the leg or shoulder, spread and flatten the meat completely.

2. In a bowl, mix cottage cheese, almonds, pistachios, morels, salt, white pepper, half the red chilli powder, garam masala, ginger and garlic pastes and the cream.

3. Spread the paste on the lamb evenly. Roll the lamb like a Swiss roll and tie firmly with a thread.

4. Place the lamb on a roasting tray, sprinkle over with salt, a pinch of garam masala, a pinch of red chilli powder, oil, crushed bayleaves, cardamom powder and cinnamon powder. Add 300-400 ml / 1 ½-2 cups of water or chicken stock.

5. Cook in a preheated oven at 175 °C / 350 °F for 45 minutes, basting every 15-20 minutes with the drippings.

6. When the lamb is completely cooked, strain the gravy from the roasting pan to a cooking vessel. Cook on low heat till it is reduced to a semi-thick sauce (about 120 ml / ⅔ cup).

7. Heat the oil in a pan, add onions, the remaining ginger and garlic pastes, diced tomatoes, garam masala, mace powder, salt, green chillies, cumin powder, green coriander and the sauce. Cook for 2-3 minutes.

8. To serve, untie the lamb, cut into thick slices and arrange on a serving dish. Pour the hot sauce over the meat and serve immediately.

Note: While rolling the meat, a hard-boiled egg can be placed in the centre.

SAAG MURGH

(Chicken in a spicy spinach purée)

Serves: 4-5   Preparation time: 10 minutes   Cooking time: 45 minutes

Ingredients

Chicken, skinned, cut into pieces *1 kg*
Spinach *(palak)*, puréed *350 gm / 1 ¾ cups*
Oil *60 ml / 4 tbsp*
Cinnamon *(dalchini)* sticks *4*
Bayleaves *(tej patta) 2*
Ginger *(adrak)* paste (p. 8) *40 gm / 2 ⅔ tbsp*
Garlic *(lasan)* paste (p. 8) *40 gm / 2 ⅔ tbsp*
Onion paste (p. 6) *200 gm / 1 cup*
Red chilli powder *10 gm / 2 tsp*
Tomatoes, chopped *180 gm / ¾ cup*
Maize flour *(makkai ka atta) 3 gm / ⅔ tsp*
Water *40 ml / 2 ⅔ tbsp*
Butter *(makhan) 100 gm / ½ cup*
Salt to taste
White pepper *(safed mirch)* powder *3 gm / ⅔ tsp*
Ginger *(adrak)* juliennes (long, thin strips) *10 gm / 2 tsp*
Fenugreek *(methi)* powder *3 gm / ⅔ tsp*

Method

1. Heat the oil in a pan; add cinnamon and bayleaves and sauté over medium heat until they begin to crackle.
2. Add the ginger, garlic and onion pastes and red chilli powder; sauté for 30-60 seconds.

3. Add tomatoes and sauté further for 1 minute.
4. Add the spinach purée, stir in maize flour mixed with water and cook over medium heat for 10-15 minutes, stirring occasionally.
5. In another pan, heat the butter and sauté the chicken until light brown.
6. Transfer the chicken pieces to the spinach sauce. Add salt and white pepper powder. Cover and simmer on very low heat (*dum*) for 10-15 minutes or till the chicken is cooked.
7. Serve, garnished with ginger juliennes and fenugreek powder.

Butter Splutter

When frying in butter, add a tablespoon of oil to the pan, to prevent the butter from burning and browning too soon.

MURGH JUGALBANDI

(Stuffed chicken breasts in a thick curry)

Serves: 4   Preparation time: 15 minutes   Cooking time: 1 hour

Ingredients

Chicken breasts *8*

For the filling:

Chicken, minced *200 gm / 1 cup*
Oil *10 ml / 2 tsp*
Mustard *(rai)* seeds *2 gm / 1/3 tsp*
Curry leaves *(meethi neem ke patte)* *2 gm / 1/3 tsp*
Salt *2 gm / 1/3 tsp*
Red chilli powder *2 gm / 1/3 tsp*
Garam masala (p. 6) *2 gm / 1/3 tsp*
Coconut *(nariyal)*, fresh, grated *10 gm / 2 tsp*
Oil for frying

For the curry:

Oil *20 ml / 4 tsp*
Cumin *(jeera)* seeds *a pinch*
Ginger-garlic *(adrak-lasan)* paste (p. 8) *10 gm / 2 tsp*
Salt to taste
Red chilli powder *2 gm / 1/3 tsp*
Turmeric *(haldi)* powder *3 gm / ½ tsp*
Coriander *(dhaniya)* powder *5 gm / 1 tsp*
Yoghurt *(dahi)* (p. 6), whisked *50 gm / 3 1/3 tbsp*
Tomato purée (p. 8) *50 gm / 3 1/3 tbsp*
Brown onion paste (p. 6) *50 gm / 3 1/3 tbsp*
Water *80 ml / 1 cup*
Tomato, diced *1*
Green peppercorns *(kachi kali mirch)* *4 gm / ¾ tsp*

Method

1. Clean and wash the chicken breasts. Make deep incisions near the bone of the chicken breasts. Keep aside.

2. Heat 10 ml oil in a pan; add mustard seeds and curry leaves and sauté for a few seconds. Add the mince and cook for about 5-6 minutes.
3. Add salt, red chilli powder, garam masala and grated coconut. Stir-cook for a few minutes. Remove from heat and keep aside to cool.
4. Stuff the chicken breasts with the prepared mixture. Heat oil in a pan, add 2 chicken breasts at a time and sauté till golden brown on both sides. Remove and keep aside.
5. For the curry, heat oil in a pan, add cumin and sauté for a few seconds. Add ginger-garlic paste and sauté for 1 minute.
6. Add salt, red chilli powder, turmeric powder and coriander powder; cook for another minute.
7. Stir in the yoghurt and tomato purée and stir-fry on medium heat. Add the brown onion paste and cook till the oil leaves the sides of the pan. Add water and bring to a boil; simmer and cook till the curry reduces to three-fourths of the original quantity.
8. Add the chicken pieces to the curry and allow to cook for 10-12 minutes. Remove from heat.
9. Carefully lift the chicken pieces from the curry and place on a serving platter. Pour the curry on top and serve hot, garnished with tomato dices and green peppercorns, accompanied by any Indian bread (pp. 104-107).

MALAI PRAWN CURRY

(Fresh prawns cooked in a creamy curry)

Serves: 4   Preparation time: 10 minutes   Cooking time: 30 minutes

Ingredients

Prawns *(jhinge)*, shelled, deveined *16*
Coconut *(nariyal)*, fresh, grated *1*
Oil *50 ml / 3 1/3 tbsp*
Ginger-garlic *(adrak-lasan)* paste (p. 8) *10 gm / 2 tsp*
Red chilli powder *5 gm / 1 tsp*
Coriander *(dhaniya)* powder *5 gm / 1 tsp*
Turmeric *(haldi)* powder *5 gm / 1 tsp*
Curry leaves *(meethi neem ke patte) 5 gm / 1 tsp*
Salt to taste
Yoghurt *(dahi)* (p. 6), whisked *50 gm / 3 1/3 tbsp*
Tomato purée (p. 8) *50 gm / 3 1/3 tbsp*
Water *200 ml / 1 cup*
Garam masala (p. 8) *2 gm / 1/3 tsp*

Method

1. Squeeze out the milk from the grated coconut and strain through a muslin cloth. Keep aside.
2. Heat oil in a pot *(handi)* and add all the ingredients except yoghurt and tomato pureé. Stir-fry for 2-3 minutes.
3. Stir in the yoghurt and tomato purée; mix well and cook for about 5-7 minutes.
4. Add prawns and stir-fry for 2-3 minutes. Add water and cook till the prawns are tender and the curry has thickened. Stir in garam masala and coconut milk.
5. Remove from heat and serve, accompanied by steamed rice.

LOBSTER CURRY

Serves: 4   Preparation time: 30 minutes   Cooking time: 30 minutes

Ingredients

Lobsters *800 gm*
Cooking oil *90 ml / ½ cup*
Onions, chopped *90 gm / ½ cup*
Ginger *(adrak)* paste (p. 8) *15 gm / 1 tbsp*
Garlic *(lasan)* paste (p. 8) *15 gm / 1 tbsp*
Green chillies chopped *4*
Red chilli powder *5 gm / 1 tsp*
Turmeric *(haldi)* powder *5 gm / 1 tsp*
Salt to taste
Tomatoes, chopped *120 gm / ¾ cup*
Coconut *(nariyal)* paste *60 gm / 4 tbsp*
Lemon juice *15 ml / 1 tbsp*
Curry leaves *(meethi neem ke patte) 10*
Green coriander *(hara dhaniya)*, chopped *3 gm / 1 tsp*

Method

1. Shell, devein, wash and cut lobsters into dices.
2. Heat oil in a pan and sauté onions till golden brown.
3. Add ginger-garlic paste and sauté.
4. Add green chillies, chilli powder, turmeric powder salt and tomatoes. Stir-cook till the masala-mix leaves the sides of the pan.
5. Add the diced lobsters. Sauté for 2-3 minutes.
6. Stir in the coconut paste. Add approximately 500 ml / 2 cups water and bring to boil.
7. Reduce flame and simmer.
8. Add lemon juice, curry leaves and cook for 2-3 minutes. Garnish with chopped coriander and serve accompanied by boiled rice.

CUCUMBER AND TOMATO RAITA

Serves: 6   Preparation time: 10 minutes

Ingredients

Yoghurt *(dahi)* (p. 6) *1 kg / 5 cups*
Salt to taste
Red chilli powder *5 gm / 1 tsp*
Cumin (*jeera*) powder, roasted *5 gm / 1 tsp*
Green coriander *(hara dhaniya)*, finely chopped *20 gm / 4 tsp*
Cucumber *(khira)*, finely chopped *100 gm / ½ cup*
Tomatoes, finely chopped *100 gm / ½ cup*
Onions, finely chopped *100 gm / ½ cup*

Method

1. Whisk yoghurt in a bowl, add salt, red chilli powder and roasted cumin powder.

2. Mix in green coriander, cucumber, tomatoes and onions.

3. Chill in a refrigerator and serve cold, as an accompaniment to any meal.

MINT RAITA

Serves: 4   Preparation time: 10 minutes

Ingredients

Yoghurt *(dahi)* (p. 6) *600 gm / 3 cups*
Mint *(pudina)* leaves, dried, crushed *75 gm / 5 tbsp*
Cumin *(jeera)* powder *3 gm / ½ tsp*

Method

1. In a bowl, whisk yoghurt along with salt and cumin powder. Add the mint leaves. Refrigerate for half an hour.

2. Sprinkle 1 tbsp mint leaves and serve as an accompaniment to any dish.

SESAME SEED AND TOMATO CHUTNEY

Serves: 4   Preparation time: 15 minutes   Cooking time: 20 minutes

Ingredients

Tomatoes, chopped *200 gm / 1 cup*
Sesame (*til*) seeds *30 gm / 2 tbsp*
Groundnut oil *(moongphali tel)*
30 ml / 2 tbsp
Onions, chopped *150 gm / 3/4 cup*
Red chilli powder *3 gm / ½ tsp*
Turmeric (*haldi*) powder
3 gm / ½ tsp
Asafoetida (*hing*) powder *a pinch*
Black gram (*chana dal*), roasted
20 gm / 4 tsp

For the tempering:

Oil *30 ml / 2 tbsp*
Red chillies, whole *5*
Curry leaves *(meethi-neem ke patte)*
10 gm / 2 tsp
Mustard (*rai*) seeds *3 gm / ½ tsp*

Method

1. Heat groundnut oil in a pan. Add onions and sauté till light brown.

2. Stir in red chilli powder, turmeric powder, asafoetida powder and sesame seeds. Stir-fry for a few minutes.

3. Add tomatoes along with black gram and cook further for 10 minutes.

4. Remove from heat and allow to cool. Blend to make a paste and remove to a bowl.

5. For the tempering, heat oil in a pan and add red chillies, curry leaves and mustard seeds. Sauté till they crackle and remove from heat.

6. Add the prepared tempering to the chutney and serve.

PUDINA PARANTHA

(Wholewheat bread flavoured with mint)

Serves: 4 Preparation time: 30 minutes Cooking time: 10 minutes

Ingredients

Wholewheat flour (*atta*)
½ kg / 2 ½ cups
Salt *5 gm / 1 tsp*
Clarified butter (*ghee*)
120 gm / ½ cup
Water *250 ml / 1 ¼ cups*
Mint (*pudina*) leaves, dried
5 gm / 1 tsp

Method

1. Mix flour, salt and half of clarified butter; add water and knead to a smooth dough. Cover and keep aside for 30 minutes.

2. Shape the dough into a ball. Flatten into a round disc with a rolling pin. Apply the remaining clarified butter and sprinkle dried mint leaves.

3. Pleat the dough into 1 collected strip. Shape into balls and roll out into 6"-diameter pancakes.

4. Heat a griddle (*tawa*) / tandoor and cook till brown spots appear on both the sides.

Taftan

Khasta Roti

Pudina Parantha

Missi Roti

TAFTAN

(Rich, leavened, rice-flour bread)

Serves: 4 Preparation time: 1 hour
Cooking time: 10 minutes

Ingredients

Rice flour (*chawal ka atta*) *480 gm / 2 ½ cups*
Salt to taste, Water
Sugar *3 gm / ½ tsp*
Milk *240 ml / 1 cup*
Clarified butter *(ghee) 180 gm / ¾ cup*
Yeast *3 gm / ½ tsp*
Melon *(magaz)* seeds *10 gm / 2 tsp*
Green coriander (*hara dhaniya*), chopped *10 gm / 2 tsp*

Method

1. Sieve flour and salt together.
2. Make a well in the flour. Add water, sugar, milk, clarified butter, yeast and melon seeds. Mix gradually and knead into a soft dough.
3. Divide into 4 equal balls and set aside for half an hour.
4. Dust lightly and roll into 3 ½" discs, ¼" thick. Sprinkle with coriander.
5. Bake in a tandoor till brown.
6. Brush with clarified butter and serve hot.

MISSI ROTI

(Flavoured gram-flour bread cooked in a tandoor)

Serves: 4 Preparation time: 30 minutes
Cooking time: 10 minutes

Ingredients

Gram flour (*besan*) *300 gm / 1 ½ cups*
Flour (*maida*) *100 gm / ½ cup*
Green chillies, chopped *25 gm / 5 tsp*
Ginger (*adrak*), chopped *25 gm / 5 tsp*

Green coriander (*hara dhaniya*),
chopped *25 gm / 5 tsp*
Pomegranate seeds (*anardana*), *20 gm / 4 tsp*
Cumin (*jeera*) seeds *15 gm / 1 tbsp*
Onion seeds (*kalonji*) *25 gm / 5 tsp*
Salt *10 gm / 2 tsp*
Butter *100 gm / ½ cup*
Clarified butter (*ghee*) *30 gm / 2 tbsp*

Method

1. Chop green chillies, ginger and coriander finely.
2. Crush pomegranate, cumin and onion seeds with a rolling pin.
3. Mix all ingredients except butter; knead to a soft dough with water.
4. Shape into balls and roll out into 6"-diameter pancakes.
5. Cook on a griddle (*tawa*) or in a tandoor until brown on both sides.
6. Remove from fire, apply butter and serve hot.

KHASTA ROTI

(Wholewheat oven-baked bread)

Serves: 4-5 Preparation time: 25 minutes Cooking time: 10-15 minutes

Ingredients

Wholewheat flour (*atta*) *500 gm / 2 ½ cups*
Salt to taste, Sugar *12 gm / 2 ½ tsp*
Carom *(ajwain)* seeds *15 gm / 1 tbsp*
Water *300 ml / 1 ½ cups*

Method

1. Sieve flour; add salt, sugar and carom seeds. Knead into a hard dough with water. Cover with a moist cloth and keep aside for 15 minutes.
2. Divide the dough into 10 balls. Dust and roll into 10 cm *rotis*. Prick with a fork evenly.
3. Bake the *rotis* in an oven at 175 °C / 350 °F for 8-10 minutes or till light brown in colour.

Glossary of Cooking Terms

Baste : Moistening meat, poultry or game during roasting by spooning over it, its juices.

Broil : Cook on a rack or on a gridiron.

Blanch : Immerse in boiling water so that the peel comes off.

Devein : Remove the main central vein from a fish.

Dice : Cut into small cubes.

Marinade : A seasoned mixture of oil, vinegar, lemon juice, etc. in which meat, poultry and fish is left for some time to soften its fibres and add flavour to it.

Parboil : Boil for part of the normal cooking time.

Sauté : Fry quickly over strong heat in fat or oil.

Simmer : Keep boiling gently on low heat.

Skewer : Fasten together pieces of food compactly on a specially designed long pin, for cooking.

Sitr-fry : Fry rapidly while stirring and tossing.

Stock : Liquid produced when meat, poultry, bones and vegetables are simmered in water with herbs and flavourings for several hours; stock forms the basis of soups, stews, etc.

Whisk : To beat air rapidly into a mixture with an egg beater, rotary beater or electric beater.

INDEX

CURRIES

Vegetarian

Non-Vegetarian

ACCOMPANIMENTS

ACKNOWLEDGEMENTS

Grateful thanks to the Master Chefs at **Hotel Holiday Inn Crowne Plaza,** New Delhi, and the **Oberoi Group of Hotels,** New Delhi, for making available their kitchens for the preparation and photography of the dishes.

ISBN: 81-7436-076-X

M 75, Greater Kailash II Market
New Delhi-110 048, INDIA
Tel.: (011) 6442271, 6462782
Fax: (011) 6467185
E-mail: rolibook@del2.vsnl.net.in

Photographs: Dheeraj Paul

Printed in Singapore